renew the. . spirit

Simply *Christmas*

201 Easy Crafts, Food and Decorating Ideas

Carol Field Dahlstrom

Brave Ink Press
Ankeny, Iowa

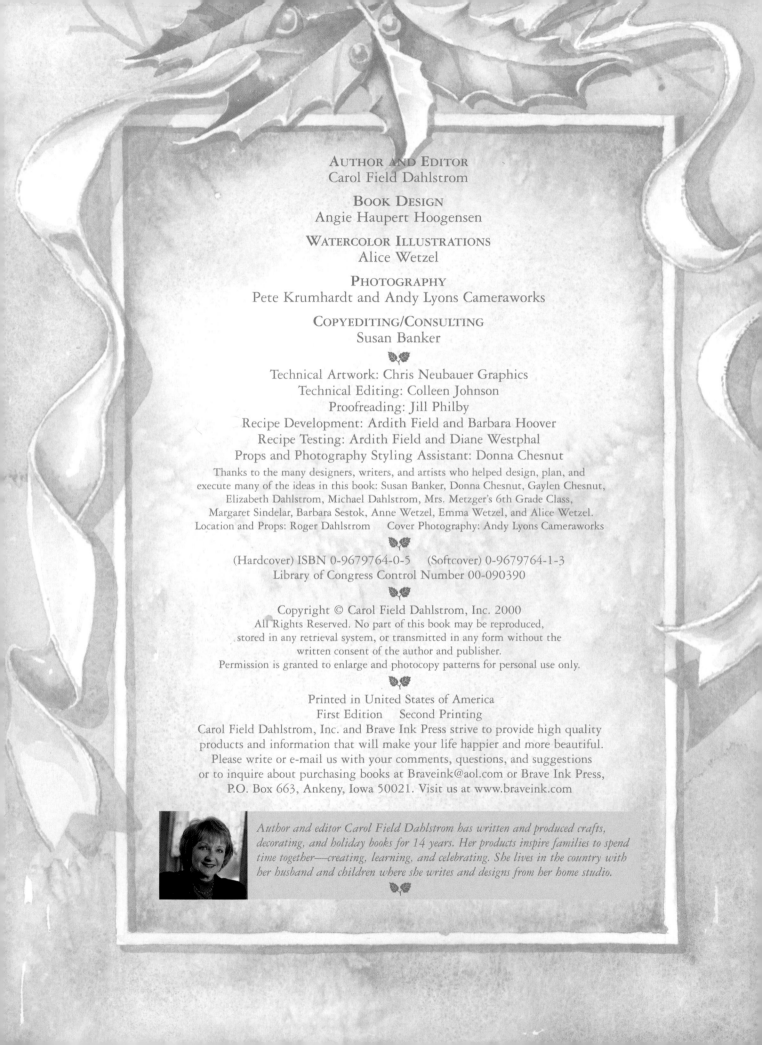

AUTHOR AND EDITOR
Carol Field Dahlstrom

BOOK DESIGN
Angie Haupert Hoogensen

WATERCOLOR ILLUSTRATIONS
Alice Wetzel

PHOTOGRAPHY
Pete Krumhardt and Andy Lyons Cameraworks

COPYEDITING/CONSULTING
Susan Banker

❧

Technical Artwork: Chris Neubauer Graphics
Technical Editing: Colleen Johnson
Proofreading: Jill Philby
Recipe Development: Ardith Field and Barbara Hoover
Recipe Testing: Ardith Field and Diane Westphal
Props and Photography Styling Assistant: Donna Chesnut

Thanks to the many designers, writers, and artists who helped design, plan, and
execute many of the ideas in this book: Susan Banker, Donna Chesnut, Gaylen Chesnut,
Elizabeth Dahlstrom, Michael Dahlstrom, Mrs. Metzger's 6th Grade Class,
Margaret Sindelar, Barbara Sestok, Anne Wetzel, Emma Wetzel, and Alice Wetzel.
Location and Props: Roger Dahlstrom   Cover Photography: Andy Lyons Cameraworks

❧

(Hardcover) ISBN 0-9679764-0-5   (Softcover) 0-9679764-1-3
Library of Congress Control Number 00-090390

❧

❧

Printed in United States of America
First Edition   Second Printing
Carol Field Dahlstrom, Inc. and Brave Ink Press strive to provide high quality
products and information that will make your life happier and more beautiful.
Please write or e-mail us with your comments, questions, and suggestions
or to inquire about purchasing books at Braveink@aol.com or Brave Ink Press,
P.O. Box 663, Ankeny, Iowa 50021. Visit us at www.braveink.com

*Author and editor Carol Field Dahlstrom has written and produced crafts,
decorating, and holiday books for 14 years. Her products inspire families to spend
time together—creating, learning, and celebrating. She lives in the country with
her husband and children where she writes and designs from her home studio.*

❧

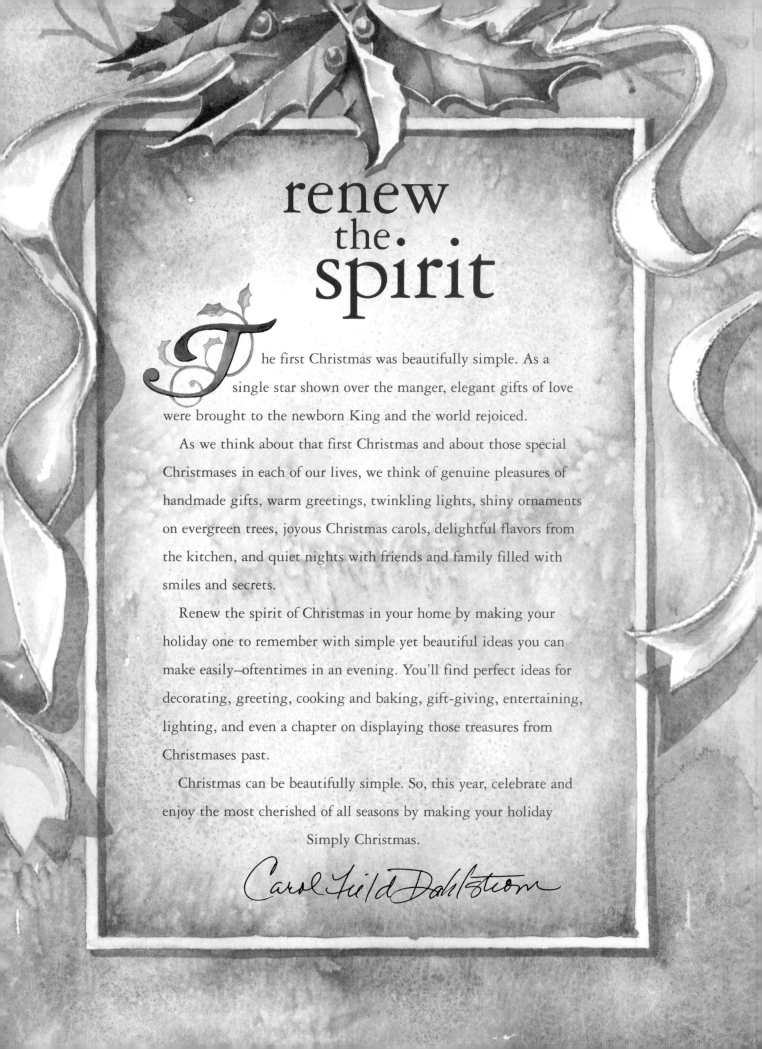

renew the. . spirit

The first Christmas was beautifully simple. As a single star shown over the manger, elegant gifts of love were brought to the newborn King and the world rejoiced.

As we think about that first Christmas and about those special Christmases in each of our lives, we think of genuine pleasures of handmade gifts, warm greetings, twinkling lights, shiny ornaments on evergreen trees, joyous Christmas carols, delightful flavors from the kitchen, and quiet nights with friends and family filled with smiles and secrets.

Renew the spirit of Christmas in your home by making your holiday one to remember with simple yet beautiful ideas you can make easily—oftentimes in an evening. You'll find perfect ideas for decorating, greeting, cooking and baking, gift-giving, entertaining, lighting, and even a chapter on displaying those treasures from Christmases past.

Christmas can be beautifully simple. So, this year, celebrate and enjoy the most cherished of all seasons by making your holiday Simply Christmas.

Carol Field Dahlstrom

contents

1

Decorate

From glittered ornaments to beaded trees, from painted sleds to smiling snowmen, you'll find easy-to-make yet stunning ideas to make your holiday decorating a pleasure for you as well as everyone who comes to call.

2

Greet

Whether you're making your own Christmas cards or giving someone a holiday telephone call, you'll want your greeting to be just perfect. You'll find projects galore in this chapter full of happy greeting ideas.

3

Nourish

Fill their hearts and their tummies with goodies from your kitchen. Whether it be a yummy pecan roll, a hearty soup, or a plate of sweet candy treats, you'll find family-tested favorites in this delicious chapter.

4

Give

Handmade gifts are the best ones of all. Whether you need a gift for a sweet baby, a bouncy teenager, a special teacher, or a dear friend, you will find the perfect gift to make in this chapter.

6

5

Entertain

Put everyone in the holiday spirit with these beautifully simple ideas for entertaining. Elegant centerpieces, memorable napkin rings, festive tabletops, and personalized tableware—you'll find this and more in this idea-filled chapter.

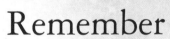

Light

Twinkling lights— whether from colorful tree bulbs or from flickering candles, always signify that Christmas is near. In this chapter you'll find bright and colorful candles, sparkling star luminarias, pretty lampshades that say "Merry Christmas," and more to light up your holiday.

7

Remember

Those treasures we've saved for years are given new life with clever ideas for displaying them. Antique card boxes, tiny celluloid reindeer, and vintage bubble lights are just a few of the things you'll find in this chapter.

About this Book

To make this book work for you and to save you time for more precious things like Christmas hugs and family gatherings, look for these icons for quick reference.

❧ Each chapter is filled with ideas you can make quickly and easily. Most of these projects can be made in an evening with just a few supplies.

This icon will indicate the materials you need to gather together to make the project.

Whenever possible, we've listed where to find the materials you'll need to make each of the projects. Many of the materials you'll have around the house and most of the other materials can be purchased at discount stores, crafts stores, or home centers.

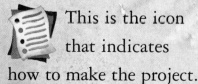 This is the icon that indicates how to make the project.

❧ Some of the projects are so easy to make you usually don't need any special materials at all. These are projects that you can make in just a few minutes—maybe after the children have gone to bed or when your husband is doing the dishes.

Look for this icon to find these quick-as-a-wink projects to make.

At the end of each chapter we've listed even more ideas and special tips for making your holiday a pleasure for you and your family.

All of the recipes in this book have come from some of the best cooks in the country—from towns and cities just like yours. These are favorite recipes from families that enjoy them year after year. All of the recipes have been made and tested to assure quality and accuracy. The recipes don't require a long shopping list, nor do they contain unusual or hard-to-find ingredients.

Look for this icon to gather the ingredients you need.

Look for this icon to find the method for making the recipe.

We know you'll love making all of the beautifully simple projects and recipes in this book, and that you'll find you still have time to spare to enjoy a very Merry Christmas.

Decorate

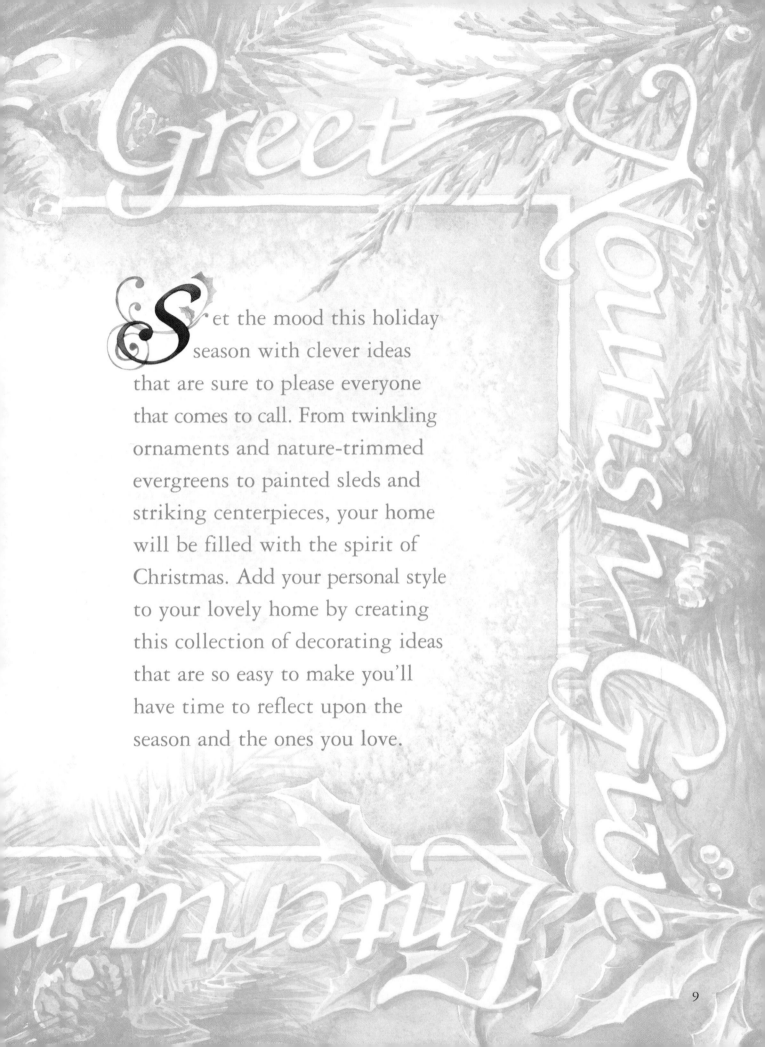

et the mood this holiday season with clever ideas that are sure to please everyone that comes to call. From twinkling ornaments and nature-trimmed evergreens to painted sleds and striking centerpieces, your home will be filled with the spirit of Christmas. Add your personal style to your lovely home by creating this collection of decorating ideas that are so easy to make you'll have time to reflect upon the season and the ones you love.

Toppers In-a-Row

Finial-type tree toppers make an elegant mantel arrangement when embellished and lined up in a row. We propped ours in various levels of glass candleholders, tied a bow at the middle, and surrounded the festive arrangement with greens and sparkling beads.

HERE'S WHAT YOU NEED

Purchased tree toppers in assorted colors
Old towel
Paint pens in desired colors
Glitter to match the topper color
Ribbon to match the topper color
Glass candleholders
Scissors
Greens
Purchased garlands of beads

HERE'S WHAT YOU DO

Lay the topper on an old towel to keep it from rolling. Draw a design on one side of the topper with the paint pen. We made swirls, dots, and curlicues.

While the paint is wet, sprinkle it with glitter. Let that side of the topper dry. Turn it over and repeat on the other side. Allow that side to dry.

Choose a ribbon that is the same color as or accents the topper. Tie a bow around the middle of the topper.

Arrange the toppers on the mantel, placing them in varied sizes of glass candleholders. Add greens and garlands of beads.

Pretty Teacup Tree

Gather all of your favorite teacups and display them beautifully by tying them on your Christmas tree. We've added delicate baby's breath and sweetheart roses to complete the beautiful tree.

HERE'S WHAT YOU NEED

Small, preferably lightweight teacups in assorted colors and sizes

1-inch-wide ribbon that ties a tight knot and bow (we used a different color on each cup)

Scissors

Sweetheart roses

Flower vials to hold water (available at floral shops)

Baby's breath

Rubber bands

HERE'S WHAT YOU DO

Choose ribbon that will not slip when tied. It will take about 1 yard of ribbon to tie a generous bow for each cup.

Thread the ribbon through the handle of the cup and tie a knot. Tie another knot to secure.

Tie the cup onto the tree by first tying a double knot on the tree branch. Then tie a pretty bow. Pull the bow tightly.

Cut the rose leaving only about a 3-inch-long stem. Slide the stem into the water vial. Arrange the baby's breath around the rose. Secure it with a rubber band.

Using another piece of ribbon, tie a knot and a bow around the rubber band.

Tuck the baby's breath and rose into the tree branches where desired around the cups.

Sparkling Ornaments

Catching the light so elegantly, these rhinestone ornaments are beautifully simple to make. Start with your favorite colored ornaments in all shapes and sizes and add the sparkle with tiny rhinestones. So easy to make, you'll want to make a set for yourself and a set for special Christmas gifts.

HERE'S WHAT YOU NEED

Solid colored ornaments in a variety of shapes (available at discount stores)
Small drinking glass
Toothpick
White crafts glue
Tweezers
Individual rhinestones in various sizes and colors (available at theatrical, fabric, or craft stores)

HERE'S WHAT YOU DO

Prop the ornament in the drinking glass to keep it from rolling. Decide on the placement of the rhinestones referring to the photographs for ideas.

Using the toothpick, put tiny drops of white glue where you want the rhinestones to be. Depending on how fast you work and how fast the glue dries, try making at least 5 or 6 dots with glue.

Using the tweezers, pick up a rhinestone and press it into the glue. Continue until all of the rhinestones are positioned on that side of the ornament. Let that side of the ornament dry.

Carefully turn over the ornament and add rhinestones to the other side. Allow to dry.

Use ornaments as desired. We have stacked antique dishes to display our finished pieces.

Happy Sled

That lonely sled can be part of the holiday fun with just a little paint and some playful designs. Search flea markets for the size and style of sled that you like. Use our patterns to create your work of art or create your own designs.

HERE'S WHAT YOU NEED

Sled; sandpaper; white primer
Red spray paint; acrylic paints in teal,
*   purple, yellow, red, orange, lime*
*   green, dark green, and cream*
Tracing paper; pencil; scissors
Flat and round paintbrushes
Medium-point black permanent marker
Clear acrylic varnish
1¹/2 yards of red cording

HERE'S WHAT YOU DO

Begin with a clean, dry sled. Sand off rough surfaces. Spray the entire sled with a paint primer spray.

Paint all metal surfaces red. If the paint oversprays onto other parts of the sled they will be covered later. Let the paint dry.

You can use the patterns we've given, *below,* or adapt the patterns to fit your sled. Trace the patterns onto tracing paper; cut them out. Do not draw around them on the sled until each background color has been painted and dried.

Paint the handle teal. Let it dry and transfer the triangle trees from the patterns you cut out. Paint the trees dark green and outline them in lime green. Paint the stars yellow. Allow to dry.

For the outside panels paint in the teal background. Let dry. Paint the wavy red edge. Let dry. Transfer the stars and paint them yellow with orange edges. Paint the middle panel purple. Let dry. Paint the yellow diamonds. To create shading, add a tiny dab of red to the corners of the yellow diamond and blend while wet.

Let dry. Transfer and paint the holly. Let dry. Add white dots to look like snow by dipping the end of a paintbrush handle in the cream paint and dotting where desired. Add yellow and red checks on sled edges. Let dry. Use a medium-point black permanent marker to outline all the black areas. Spray the sled with clear acrylic varnish. Let dry. Add a length of cord through the holes in the handle.

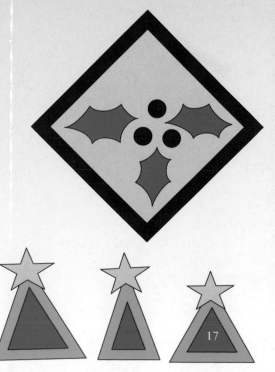

Star Attraction

It's always fun to think of just the right topper for that stately evergreen. Whether you usually have a star at the top of your holiday tree or not, this one is sure to please you.

Made from bottle-brush trees, available at discount and craft stores, this topper becomes a much talked about addition to your Christmas tree. Make smaller versions of this clever star for ornaments and for holiday gifts.

HERE'S WHAT YOU NEED
Five 3¹/₂-inch-high bottle-brush trees
Hot-glue gun and hot-glue sticks
1¹/₂-inch-diameter foam ball, such as Styrofoam
Thirteen ¹/₂-inch-diameter round, plastic ornaments
Metallic gold chenille stem

HERE'S WHAT YOU DO
Remove tree bases by turning counterclockwise.

Place a small amount of hot glue onto the bottom stem of a bottle-brush tree. Poke the stem into the foam ball and push until the stem is completely into the ball. Continue adding trees in this manner, placing each one next to the last to create a star shape.

Glue plastic ornaments over the center of the star, covering the foam ball. Build up layers to add dimension, if desired.

Fold the chenille stem in half, twisting together 2 inches from the ends. Twist ends around the tip of one bottle-brush tree for the hanger.

It's-All-in-the-Game Tree

Have the children help you round up all of those extra game pieces and use them to decorate a special Christmas tree in the game room this year. We've combined checkers, dice, board game pieces, and more to make this tree the talk of family game night.

HERE'S WHAT YOU DO

For playing cards and other paper items, punch holes on sides with a paper punch. Using the red string, weave the cards together. For items that need to be drilled, drill the sides or ends with a 1/4-inch drill bit. Connect with string in the same way. For the dice, drill and string vertically to look like icicles.

For the star at the top, glue playing cards to the piece of cardboard. Draw around a large star cookie cutter (or use a smaller cookie cutter and enlarge on the copy machine). Trace around that pattern onto the cards glued to the cardboard and cut out the star. Prop in top of tree for topper. Display on an old checkerboard.

HERE'S WHAT YOU NEED

Old game pieces such as dice, dominoes, checkers, playing cards, and board game pieces
Paper punch
Red string
Drill with 1/4-inch drill bit
Hot-glue gun and hot-glue sticks
Cardboard
Star cookie cutter
White crafts glue

Polka Dot Ornaments

So quick to make yet so elegant to display, these polka dot ornaments are sure to bring "oohs and ahs" from family and friends. Just a little bit of glue and sparkling glitter transform ordinary ornaments into beautiful decorations you'll look forward to year after year.

HERE'S WHAT YOU NEED
White crafts glue
Disposable foam plate
Pencil with new eraser
Plain-colored ornaments
Glitter to match color of ornament
Drinking glass (to hold ornament)

HERE'S WHAT YOU DO
Pour a little glue onto the disposable plate. Using the eraser end of the pencil, dip the eraser into the glue. Dot the glue onto the ornament. Repeat until you have about ten dots.

Sprinkle the wet glue with glitter. Carefully put the ornament into the glass to dry. After it is dry repeat for the other side.

Display the ornaments on a tree, on a mantel, or prop them in a glass candelabra.

Dip the eraser end of the pencil in glue and dot on the ornament.

Dust with glitter and prop in a drinking glass to allow to dry. Repeat for the other side.

Beads and Roses Garland

QUICK AS A WINK

For an elegant garland that only takes minutes to make, thread white waxed dental floss in a narrow-eyed needle. Start by stringing a bead on the end. Go through the same bead again forming a knot. Now, string beads (we used seed beads interspersed with larger marbled beads), fresh rose heads, and small Christmas ornaments in any order you choose. Make enough garland for your tree, or make a short section for a mantle trim. Tie a bead at the finished end.

Celebrate Nature Tree

Using the beauty of nature and a little paint, these ornaments and garlands make Mother Nature the star. We've used pinecones, sticks, seed pods, leaves, and acorns to create this natural beauty to enjoy for the holiday season.

HERE'S WHAT YOU NEED FOR THE PAINTED LEAVES AND MILKPODS

Scissors for clipping weeds

Milkweed pods

Acorns

Leaves

Heavy book

Newspaper

Spray paints in gold and silver

Metallic spray paints in red, yellow, green, purple, and blue (we used model car hobby paints found at hobby and craft stores)

White crafts glue

Gold or natural raffia

HERE'S WHAT YOU DO FOR THE PAINTED LEAVES AND MILKPODS

Have fun gathering nature items for this spectacular tree. When the leaves begin to turn and fall start collecting. Use your imagination, and look for anything that can be painted and used as decoration. We found these drying milkweed pods and cut them from their stem. We gathered acorns and drying leaves. Choose leaves that are a bit dry, but not too crisp or brittle.

Lay the leaves under a heavy weight such as a book and dry overnight to flatten. They will be easier to handle and easier to paint. Clean out any seeds remaining inside the milkpods.

Lay leaves and milkpods on newspaper. Spray them all with gold or silver metallic paint. Let the paint dry, turn over, and spray on the other side. Spray until

continued on page 28

27

Newspapers

Foam block, such as Styrofoam

Twigs

*Metallic spray paints in gold, green,
plum, red, blue, and other desired
colors (we used model car hobby
paints found at hobby and craft
stores)*

Twig cutter

Hot-glue gun and hot-glue sticks

Gold crafting wire

**HERE'S WHAT YOU DO
FOR THE TWIG STARS**

completely covered with paint. The
gold and silver color becomes the
base coat for the leaves.

Add another color of spray paint
over the gold and silver leaves.
Very lightly spray colors such as
green, red, purple, and yellow over
the gold leaves. Do not spray them
heavily. Some of the gold should
show through.

Try spraying more than one
color on a leaf. For example, spray
part of a leaf red and spray the rest
of it yellow. The sprays will
overlap each other and make a very
pretty combination of color.
Experiment with combining
colors. Spraying yellow over green
or red makes a very brilliant color.
Colors like blue and purple look
good over the silver leaves. Paint
all leaves as you wish, let them dry,
turn them over, and paint the
other side.

Spray the acorns in bright colors
such as blue, green, purple, red,
and yellow. Paint them solid, or
paint the cap one color and the
base another color.

When the acorns are dry, glue
them into the milkweed pods
tucked in towards the top. Let the
glue dry.

Tie the painted nature trims
with a generous piece of gold
colored raffia. If you cannot find
gold raffia, simply spray a bundle
of raffia with gold spray paint
and let dry.

In a well-ventilated area, cover
work surface with newspapers.
Place the foam block in the center
of the newspapers. Poke sticks into
foam to stand them upright.

Spray the sticks with gold spray
paint. Let the paint dry. Lightly

HERE'S WHAT YOU DO
FOR THE GARLAND

In a well-ventilated area, cover work surface with newspapers. Place the nature items in the center of the newspapers.

Spray the acorns and pinecones with gold spray paint. Let the paint dry. Turn and repeat. Lightly spray the top surfaces of the items with a colored spray paint. Let dry.

To paint the sticks, poke them into foam to stand them upright. Spray the sticks with colored spray paint. Let dry.

Use a drill to drill holes through the center of each acorn. Drill holes through each stick, drilling several holes about 1-inch apart. Cut the twigs between the drilled holes.

Decide on the sequence and begin threading painted nature items on wire. To add a pinecone, wrap wire around the center on the pinecone. Continue threading on items until the desired length is reached.

spray one side of each stick with a colored spray paint. Let dry.

Cut twigs into various lengths between 5 and 10 inches. Arrange five sticks to form a star, leaving a longer twig trailing at the bottom. Glue the intersections.

Use 12-inch lengths of wire to wrap the outer intersections, covering the glue. Tuck the wire ends into the wraps.

Cut a 6-inch piece of wire for the hanger. Thread it through the wires at the top of the star. Twist the ends to secure.

HERE'S WHAT YOU NEED
FOR THE GARLAND

Newspapers

Acorns, twigs, and pinecones

Metallic spray paints in gold, green, plum, red, blue, and other desired colors (we used model car hobby paints found at hobby and craft stores)

Foam block, such as Styrofoam

Drill with ⅛-inch bit

Twig cutter

Gold crafting wire

29

Window Dress Ups

QUICK AS A WINK

Try unexpected holiday trims to dress up your curtains or
drapes for Christmas. We added fresh greens to a small
purchased berry wreath and then pulled our curtain through
the center, *above*. Spray painted pinecones or glittered bells,
opposite, were combined with twisted ribbon to make festive
Christmas window trims.

31

Beaded Tree Trio

Standing so stately and tall this beaded trio will become the center of attention. Line the trees on the mantle or use as a centerpiece for your holiday table.

Here's What You Need

Plastic cones, such as Styrofoam in 9, 11, and 13-inch heights

Wrapping paper in similar color as beads

White crafts glue; straight pins; scissors

Three 12-inch long pieces of ⁵/₈-inch dowel

White acrylic paint; paintbrush

Tracing paper; pencil

Two 12×18×1-inch sheets of plastic foam such as Styrofoam; sharp knife

3 small dimensional plastic foam stars

White iridescent glitter

Three 3¹/₂-inch-squares of cardboard

Beaded garlands in desired colors

Curling ribbon

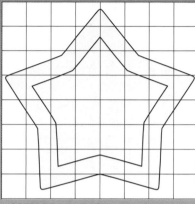

Here's What You Do

Cover each cone with wrapping paper by spreading glue around the cone and rolling the paper around it. Trim excess paper. Fold the paper neatly onto the bottom of the cone and glue in place. Use straight pins to hold in place while glue dries. Remove pins when dry.

Pierce a hole in bottom of cone and paper with the pointed end of scissors. Paint the dowel with white acrylic paint. Let dry. Push the dowel into the cone until there is 5 inches of dowel remaining out of the bottom of the cone. Reinforce the dowel using crafts glue if needed.

Enlarge the star patterns, *above*, onto tracing paper or enlarge 400% on a copy machine. Cut out and trace onto flat sheet of 1-inch plastic foam. Cut out stars with sharp knife. Glue the stars together with a generous amount of crafts glue centering the smaller star on top of the larger star.

Brush a thin layer of crafts glue onto the stacked stars and onto the dimensional stars

1 SQUARE = 1 INCH

for the top of tree. Dust white iridescent glitter on all stars. Let dry.

Push the dowel end of the tree into the center of the starred tree base. Push it through both layers so it is visible on the bottom side. Reinforce the hole with a generous amount of crafts glue. To make the bottom more stable, glue the 3¹/₂-inch square of cardboard to the bottom of the stars.

Make stripes of glue around the cone from top to bottom, covering the bottom half to start. Begin attaching the strands of beads around the cone beginning at the bottom and winding upward. Hold beads in place with straight pins. Remove the pins when the glue is dry and beads are firmly in place. Tie curling ribbon just under the tree top star and let drape downward.

Vintage Look-a-Likes

QUICK AS A WINK

Vintage ornaments can be more than a treasure to enjoy each year. They can also be an inspiration to create new ones for your holiday tree. Choose ornaments that have easy designs such as the ones shown here. We've used permanent markers (they come in all colors including metallics) and glitter to reinvent these beautiful old pieces.

Simple Silvery Trims

Reminiscent of Victorian ornaments, these simple star trims are easy to make and add sparkle to any holiday tree. We've chosen to put our shimmering stars on a white feather tree keeping the look clean and fresh.

HERE'S WHAT YOU NEED
Star cookie cutters in various sizes
Silver chenille stems
Scissors; fine silver wire
Small round silver ornaments

HERE'S WHAT YOU DO
Lay the cookie cutter on a flat surface such as a table or cutting board. Wrap the chenille stem around the cookie cutter fitting it around the cookie cutter to form the star shape. Twist the chenille stem at the top to secure. Slide the star shape off of the cookie cutter.

Slip a piece of the fine silver wire through the small round ornament. Loop it up and around the top of the star. Form a hanger with another piece of a chenille stem at the top.

Hang these simple trims on a Christmas tree or in a window to catch the winter light.

Tasseled Newel Post

QUICK AS A WINK

Purchased tassels, upholstery cording, and fresh greens all combine to dress up this banister in holiday style. You can use tasseled cording that is premade, or hot glue the tassels to the ends of the cording as we did. Simply tie the cording around the newel post and tuck in some fresh greens.

Smiling Snowmen

These happy tumbling snowmen are sure to bring smiles to everyone that meets them. Made from soft clay, paint, and glitter, each snowman trim has a personality of its own. Make the little guys with clay, just as you would with snow in three parts and with lots of winter imagination.

HERE'S WHAT YOU NEED

Soft white clay (we used Crayola®
*   Model Magic®)*
Purchased Christmas ornaments
*   in desired colors*
Acrylic paints in desired colors
Fine line black permanent marker
Iridescent glitter
White crafts glue

HERE'S WHAT YOU DO

Build your tiny snowmen using the white clay. We started with two balls of clay (about the size of a grape) and added two feet. Add hats, scarves, or whatever accessories you might put on a real snowman. Fit the clay snowman onto the ornament as if it is hugging the ball or climbing on it.

Let the clay dry on the ornament. This will take about two hours. The clay will stick to the ornament until it is dry. Then it will fall away from the ornament.

Paint the snowman accessories with desired colors. Add details with the marker. While the paint is wet, sprinkle snowman with glitter. Let it dry. Glue the snowmen to the ornaments. Mix glue and water together in equal parts and paint on the white part of the snowman. Dust with glitter.

Glittering Cattails

Bring the beauty of nature into your holiday decorating by creating this beautiful arrangement made from painted cattails and fresh greens. Choose a container that complements your color scheme and display the arrangement as a centerpiece or as an entry bouquet. Tie a sheer bow of color and a special ornament around the top of the container.

HERE'S WHAT YOU NEED
Cattails
Decoupage medium
Small paintbrush
Glitter in desired color
Greens
Large vase or pail
Ribbon
Christmas ornament

HERE'S WHAT YOU DO
To make the cattails glitter, paint a coat of decoupage medium on the cattail head. Sprinkle glitter on the head and let it dry. The decoupage medium will also act as a sealant and prevent the heads from popping. Arrange the cattails with greens in a large vase or pail. (We used balsam greens with tiny blue berries in a blue sap bucket.)

Tie a ribbon and an ornament around the container. You can add water to the container to keep the greens fresher, but the cattails require no water.

This arrangement makes a beautiful centerpiece, a lovely focal point on a mantel, or a welcoming front step decoration.

Children at Peace Tree

This year bring all the children together for the holidays by creating this Children at Peace Tree. *Hand-in-Hand Garlands*, colorful *Painted Globe Ornaments, Around the World Trims*, ribbons, and oversized daisies secured in their own water containers make this tree one the whole family will love. We've topped our tree with a purchased artificial dove.

HERE'S WHAT YOU NEED FOR THE HAND-IN-HAND GARLAND
White cardstock paper (one 8¹/₂×11-inch sheet makes two paper children)
Crayons, markers, colored pencils
Scissors
Paper punch
Thin ribbon (we used ¹/₄-inch-wide ribbon)

HERE'S WHAT YOU DO FOR THE HAND-IN-HAND GARLAND
Trace the patterns on *page 45*. Take them to a copy center and have them reproduced on white cardstock paper. Give each child a boy or girl to color as they wish. When they are finished, punch a small hole in the hands of the paper doll about ¹/₄ inch from the edge. Lay the boy and girl dolls on a table, arranging them as desired. Tie the hands together using the thin ribbon.

continued on page 44

PAINTED GLOBE ORNAMENT

HERE'S WHAT YOU NEED FOR THE PAINTED GLOBE ORNAMENTS

*Clear ornaments with removable tops
(available at craft and
discount stores)*
*Acrylic paints in green, yellow, blue,
and brown*
Small plastic disposable cups

HERE'S WHAT YOU NEED FOR THE AROUND THE WORLD TRIMS

Old maps
*3-inch plastic foam ball, such as
Styrofoam*
Decoupage medium; paintbrush
Colored paper clip
Clothes hanger
Thin ribbon

AROUND THE WORLD TRIM

HERE'S WHAT YOU DO FOR THE PAINTED GLOBE ORNAMENTS

Take off the top of the ornament. Carefully drop in a drop of green, yellow, blue, and brown paint. If the paint is too thick, thin slightly with water. Swirl the paint around inside the ornament until it begins to look like a globe. Then prop the ornament in the disposable cup and let it dry. It will take a day or two to dry completely. However, you can use a hair dryer to speed up the process. After the ornament is dry, put the top back on.

HERE'S WHAT YOU DO FOR THE AROUND THE WORLD TRIMS

Tear the map into pieces about the size of a dime. Paint the decoupage medium onto the ball and place the map piece on top of the liquid. Paint over the map piece. Continue adding and overlapping pieces until the entire ball is covered. Open up the paper clip and push it into the ball. Hang the ball by the clip on a clothes hanger to dry. After the ornament is dry, cover it again with another coat of decoupage medium. Allow to dry. Tie a tiny bow at the base of the paper clip.

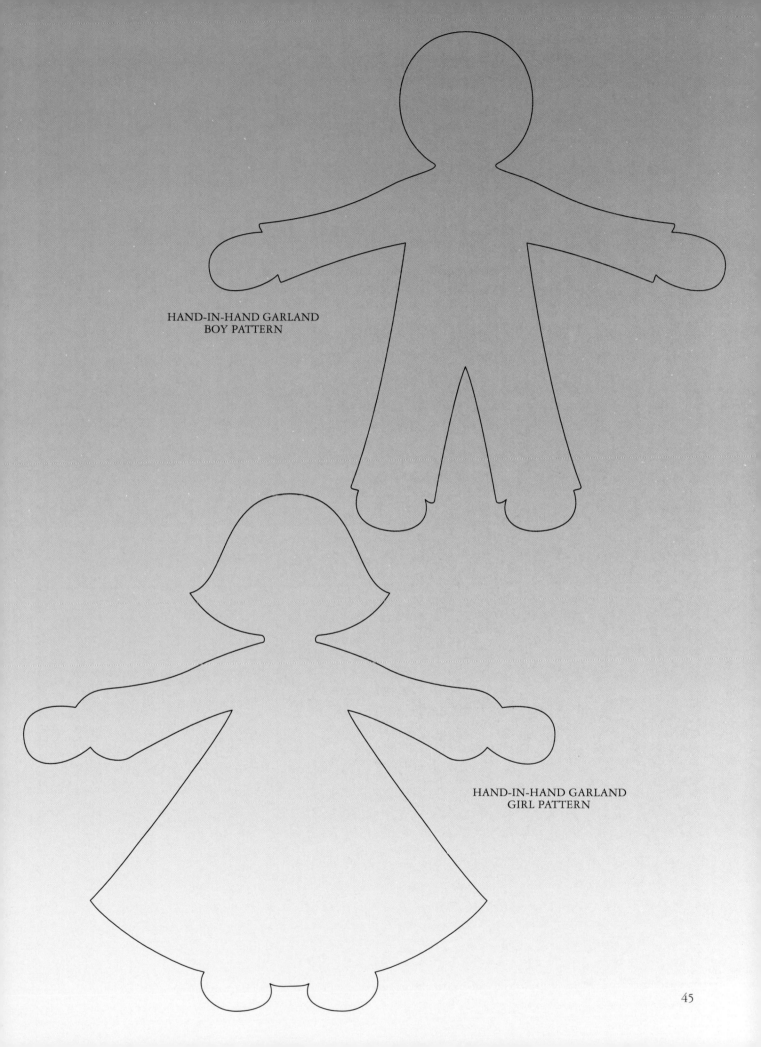

HAND-IN-HAND GARLAND
BOY PATTERN

HAND-IN-HAND GARLAND
GIRL PATTERN

Snowcapped Pinecones

Dipped in wax and dusted with glitter, these ordinary pinecones become works of art. We've stacked these pure-white beauties in an antique glass dish and added a touch of fresh holiday greenery.

HERE'S WHAT YOU NEED

White candle wax (available at craft and hobby stores)
Empty metal can (such as a vegetable can)
Old saucepan
Hot plate or stove
Small and medium sized pinecones
Fine wire
Pan or dish of cold water
Waxed paper
White glitter

HERE'S WHAT YOU DO

Break up the wax and put in the empty can. You can break the wax using a hammer and chisel or put it in a paper sack and drop it on a cement driveway or sidewalk. Fill the saucepan about 1/3 full with water. Put the can with the wax in it in the water and heat the water to boiling. The wax will melt slowly. Watch it carefully.

NEVER put the wax on the stove directly and never leave the wax unattended. As soon as it is melted turn off the stove or hot plate. Leave the can in the water.

Loop the wire around the pinecone. Dip it into the wax. Now, dip it in the cold water. Keep dipping back and forth until the pinecone has a snowy effect. (This will take from 5 to 10 dippings). Lay the pinecone on the waxed paper and dust with glitter while it is still warm. Allow to dry completely.

Using the wire as a holder, dip the pinecone in the wax.

After dipping the pinecone in the wax, dip it into the cold water. Repeat back and forth from hot wax to cold water until the cone looks frosty.

Banister Beauty

QUICK AS A WINK

Strings of beaded garlands are readily available at crafts and discount stores in every color. We decorated this banister by cutting the beads to the desired length and knotting and draping them over the railing. The final touch was added by tying a knot with the beads around the newel post.

More Ways to
Decorate

There's so much decorating you want to do and so little time. Here are some tips to save time, so you can relax and enjoy it all.

🌿 Make the newel post the center of attention by tying a single bow of elegant ribbon around it and adding a favorite ornament in the center.

🌿 Use clear storage boxes for storing ornaments and other decorations. This will take the guesswork out of finding your favorite items next year.

🌿 Display beautiful items found at holiday time in unexpected places. Ribbon candy displayed in an antique clear dish, or golden tinsel strung above a doorway adds the perfect festive touch.

🌿 Flea market finds can be the answer when searching for containers to hold holiday bouquets and arrangements. Look for silver serving pieces, old drawers, baskets, and wood bowls.

🌿 Tuck sprigs of fresh evergreen all through

the house, around clocks and pictures, in vases, and on bookshelves.

🍂 Holiday fabrics can add a splash of color when turned into no-sew tablerunners, napkins, tree skirts, and torn-fabric bows.

🍂 For kitchen fun, place holiday cookie cutters in a large, clear-glass jar tied with a ribbon or display clear red cookie cutters in the window.

🍂 Replace throw rugs with holiday-themed ones. You can find a large selection at home and discount stores.

🍂 Visit flea markets and antiques shops to find holiday postcards. Incorporate the miniature pieces of art into your decorating.

🍂 Create holiday cheer in unexpected places like the bedroom and bathroom. Look for holiday soaps, towels, sheets, and more in home decor stores.

🍂 If you absolutely love the smell of fresh evergreen, then real greens are a must. However, there are wonderful artificial greens that work well for wrapping banisters and pillars. Wait until after Christmas and buy the best possible quality when it is on sale for next year's decorating.

🍂 Spray-paint large terra-cotta pots bright gold and fill with pinecones and the tops of real evergreens for festive walkway decorations.

Decorate

Remember

Greet

Light

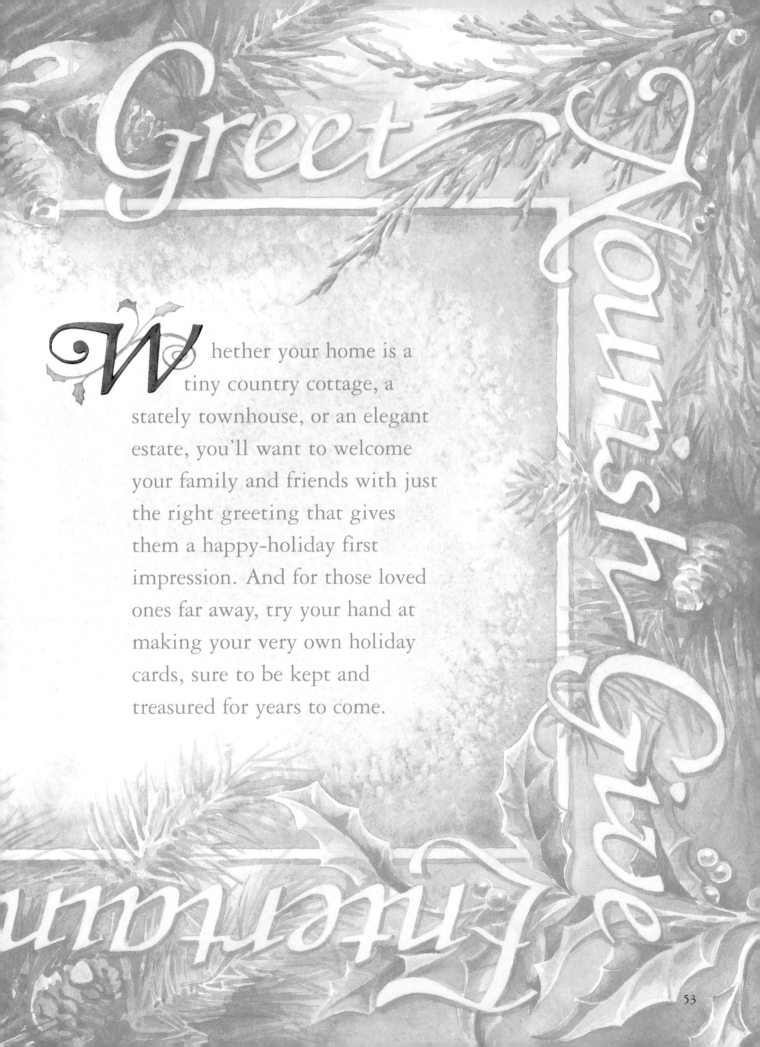

Whether your home is a tiny country cottage, a stately townhouse, or an elegant estate, you'll want to welcome your family and friends with just the right greeting that gives them a happy-holiday first impression. And for those loved ones far away, try your hand at making your very own holiday cards, sure to be kept and treasured for years to come.

Friendly Winter Hello

Send those holiday greetings by telephone this year, and this oh-so-pretty snowflake-covered phone will put you in the holiday spirit. We've decorated this purchased telephone with delicate snowflakes using a fine-line paint marker.

We've given some patterns for you to follow, but remember, no two snowflakes are ever alike!

HERE'S WHAT YOU NEED

Purchased telephone (we chose black in a classic style, but choose a phone that suits your holiday decor)
White chalk
Fine-line permanent paint markers in gold and white or desired colors

HERE'S WHAT YOU DO

Be sure that the phone is clean and dry. With a piece of white chalk, mark a dot where you want to place your snowflakes. You can vary the size of the snowflakes, and group some if you wish.

Using the fine-line permanent marker and the patterns, *below*, as inspiration, draw the snowflakes on the telephone. Place them on all areas of the phone varying the size and color. Wait for each area to dry before proceeding to another area.

Dainty Doily Cards

All dressed up in baubles and lace, these sweet and beautiful Christmas cards will be treasured for years to come. The velum paper and silver tones of the charms make the cards ring with elegant holiday cheer.

HERE'S WHAT YOU NEED FOR THE BLUE CARD

6¹/₄×9¹/₂-inch piece of
    medium-weight blue paper
6×9-inch piece of velum
Decorative-edge scissors
6-inch-high white paper
    heart-shape doily
Ruler; glue stick
18-inch piece of 1-inch-wide sheer
    blue ribbon
Silicone glue
5 silver snowflake charms

HERE'S WHAT YOU DO FOR THE BLUE CARD

Fold the blue piece of paper in half, and the velum in half aligning the short ends. Trim one short end of velum using decorative-edge scissors. Fold paper doily horizontally, 3¹/₄ inches above the point. Use a glue stick to adhere it onto the blue paper, aligning the folds. Let the glue dry.

Place the velum over the blue card, aligning the folds with the decorative-edge on the front. Tie the paper layers together using ribbon. Tie a bow at the top center.

Use silicone glue to attach the snowflake charms evenly spaced across the card front, ¹/₂ to ³/₄ inch from bottom edge. Let glue dry.

HERE'S WHAT YOU NEED FOR THE WHITE CARD

4³/₄×7¹/₂-inch piece of
    medium-weight white paper
4³/₄×7¹/₂-inch piece of velum
A 6-inch round, plastic lid
Pencil; scallop-edge scissors
Ruler; glue stick
4-inch-diameter silver doily
White sewing thread; needle
Silver snowflake charm
Narrow silver cord
Silver marking pen; envelope

HERE'S WHAT YOU DO FOR THE WHITE CARD

Fold white paper and velum in half, aligning short ends. To round one end of the velum, trace around a plastic lid. Cut along the pencil line using scallop-edge scissors. Place the velum over the white card, aligning the folds. The side with the decorative-edge will be the front. Use a glue stick to adhere the layers on the back. Let dry.

Fold the paper doily 2³/₄ inches from one edge. Use a glue stick to adhere to the velum, aligning the folds. Let the glue dry. Use needle and thread to sew snowflake charm to card front, just below the fold. Sew center of cord to top of the charm. Tie the cord into a bow. Add white paint dots to the doily edge and to the velum paper.

Pretty and Pink Poinsettia Wreath

Here's What You Need

1 yard each of dark and light pink felt

Straight pins

16-inch plastic foam such as Styrofoam flat wreath

Scissors

Tracing paper

Pencil

Gold chenille pipe cleaners

Gold artificial seeded stems (available at crafts or discount stores in the floral department)

Wire hanger for hanging

Here's What You Do

Cut 2-inch strips from the ends of felt pieces. Wrap the wreath with the strips to cover the foam. Pin in place. Enlarge and trace the patterns, *below*, onto tracing paper and cut out. Draw around patterns on the felt. Use four petals for each size bloom. We used 13 blooms of various sizes to cover our wreath. Fold each felt petal in half lengthwise. Fold the edge back to the middle in an accordion pleating fashion. Pinch at center and secure with a chenille stem. Twist the stem around a small piece of the purchased gold seeds to form a center. Bring ends of the chenille stem around to the back and poke through to the wreath base. Continue making blooms and covering the wreath. Add a wire hanger to the back for hanging.

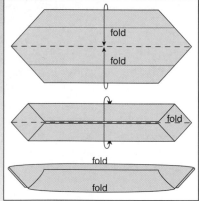

FOLDING DIAGRAM

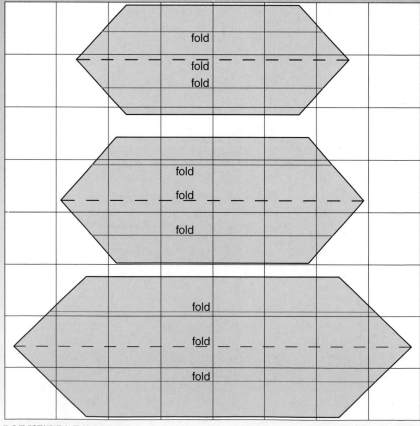

POINSETTIA PATTERNS

1 SQUARE = 1 INCH

We took this
age-old method
for making blooms
a step further by using
beautifully colored felt so
available today. Adding a
golden seed-like center
creates just the right
combination for providing
a soft and warm greeting
for your holiday guests.

Stamped Greetings

With all the beautiful printing stamps available today, we sometimes forget that we can create our own in minutes using something as simple as a potato. This often-used stamping process holds the paint well and lends itself to so many variations. Try our design or one of your own to say "Merry Christmas" this year.

HERE'S WHAT YOU NEED
Large potato
Small sharp paring knife; paper towel
Assorted color paper scraps
Acrylic paints in green and rust red
Disposable foam plate
Scissors, including decorative edge scissors
Glue stick
Card stock (available at crafts stores)
Embellishments such as buttons,
   jewels, beads, and ribbons
Thick white crafts glue

HERE'S WHAT YOU DO
Wash and dry the potato. Slice the potato in half. Be careful to slice evenly so the sliced side lays flat.

Using a small sharp paring knife, cut a design into the potato. Draw the design first with a pencil and put an X on the areas you will be cutting away. We made a simple triangle shape for a tree, and added a rectangular tree base. Cut into the potato at least 1/8 inch around the basic tree shape. Then cut from outer edge of potato inward to the outline of the shape. Remove extra potato from the tree shape, leaving tree intact. Cut horizontal lines across the tree. Cut them at an angle to make a V-cut. Remove those pieces. Dab off extra moisture from the potato with a paper towel.

Gather an assortment of papers and begin stamping on the papers. Spread a thin coat of paint on the plate, dip the potato in the paint, and stamp onto the papers.

After you've stamped a number of pieces, choose the ones you like best and cut or tear them out. Tear your papers into rectangular

Cut the edges of the potato away leaving the desired shape.

Put the paint on the plate and dip the potato into the paint. Print on desired papers adjusting the amount of paint as needed.

shapes or cut them with decorative scissors. Layer the stamped pieces onto a contrasting paper with torn edges. Apply glue stick to the back of papers to affix to each other. Mount onto a piece of card stock or purchased plain card in a coordinating color.

Decorate the cards with buttons, jewels, ribbons, beads, or anything you wish attaching the embellishments with a small dab of crafts glue.

Happy Holidays Mailbox

What better way to say welcome than a happily painted mailbox. We sponge painted this one first and then added a happy holiday greeting with stars outlined in sparkling gold paint.

HERE'S WHAT YOU NEED
Purchased metal mailbox
Spray primer
Acrylic paints in purple, teal, green, red, bright aqua, and hot pink
Small sea sponge and water
Disposable foam plate
Tracing paper
Pencil; scissors
Four 1/2-inch-thick kitchen sponges
Large tip gold paint marker
12×12-inch piece of 1/8-inch fir plywood; saw
Weather-resistant glue
Varnish or sealer

HERE'S WHAT YOU DO
Prime the mailbox with a spray primer. Let dry.

Gather the colors of paint together you wish to use. We used purple, hot pink, red, teal, bright aqua, and green acrylic paints.

Soak the small natural sea sponge in water. Squeeze out excess water. Place a generous amount of paint on the disposable plate. Dab sponge in the first color of paint. (We used purple.) Sponge an area in a random swirly pattern at one end. Before the paint dries, add another color (we used teal) sponging and blending the purple and teal. Continue to add other colors (we used green next to the teal, magenta next to purple, and red next to magenta). Continue to paint quickly working while the colors are all still wet. Let the paint dry.

continued on page 64

Happy Holidays Mailbox – continued

Trace the sponge star patterns, *opposite*, onto tracing paper, cut out and trace each one onto a 1/2-inch flat sponge. Save the patterns. Cut out the star shapes from the sponge, soak in water and squeeze out the excess water. Spread a generous amount of paint, (we

used aqua or hot pink) onto the disposable plate. Press the star shaped sponge into the paint and stamp onto the mailbox. Make small and large pink and aqua stars randomly. Let the paint dry.

Outline the stamped stars with a wide tip gold paint pen. Let dry.

Place the smaller tissue star pattern over the top of the larger painted one skewed at an angle and trace around it with gold paint marker. Let the marker dry.

Repeat by placing the tissue patterns over the painted stars and drawing around them with the paint marker.

To make the star flag we used the plastic flag that came with the mailbox. Cut off the flag portion and paint the flag stem.

Trace the wood star patterns *opposite*, onto 1/8-inch-thick wood. Cut one large star and two smaller ones. Paint the center large star gold on both sides. Paint each small star in pinks. Sponge them in the same manner as the mailbox. Sponge magenta around the edges and lighter pink towards the center. Let dry.

Glue the three stars together with the gold one sandwiched in the middle.

Glue the painted star onto the flag using weather-resistant glue. Paint a coat of varnish or sealer over the entire mailbox to prevent weathering if the mailbox will be used outside.

1 *Using the natural sponge, sponge on the base color of the paint using a circular motion. Let the paint dry.*

2 *Use the kitchen sponge cut in the shape of a star to sponge over the other paint. Let the paint dry.*

3 *Draw around the star with a gold paint marker. Let the marker dry.*

4 *Place the other star pattern askew over the drawn star and mark the points. Trace over with gold marker.*

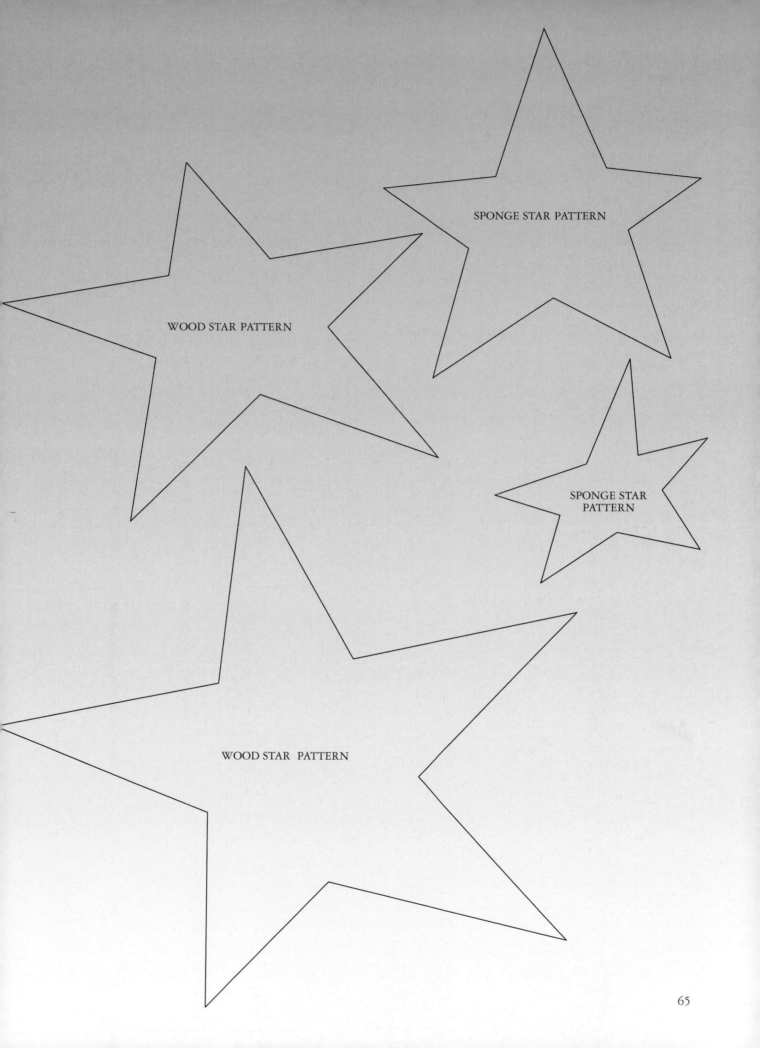

SPONGE STAR PATTERN

WOOD STAR PATTERN

SPONGE STAR
PATTERN

WOOD STAR PATTERN

65

Traditional Welcome Wreath

Traditional fruit motifs have served as a sign of holiday welcomes for generations. The range of hues and shapes that the fruit offers yields wonderful combinations of texture and color. This showy beaded fruit wreath combines the glorious colors of nature yet is so easy to make. The purchased beaded fruits are inexpensive and easy to find at crafts and discount stores.

This wreath will last for years and can be brought out Christmas after Christmas to greet friends and neighbors.

Here's What You Need
12-inch plastic foam wreath (such as Styrofoam) with flat edges
About 30 artificial magnolia leaves
Hot-glue gun and hot-glue sticks
Purchased beaded fruit with plastic foam core (available at crafts and discount stores) we chose peaches, red and green apples, oranges, and pears
Saw (we used a band saw) Note: If you don't have a band saw, take the fruit to your hardware or home center and ask them to cut the artificial fruit for you. They may charge a minimal fee
Protective goggles
Thin wire for hanging

Here's What You Do
Arrange the leaves on the wreath. Overlap the leaves to cover all of the foam wreath. Hot-glue in place overlapping the leaves as you glue.

Cut the fruit in half using a band saw. Most beaded fruit have a plastic core and are fairly easy to cut. Wear protective goggles because the tiny beads can fly off when cutting.

Arrange the fruit over the leaves. Hot-glue in place.

Make a loop from the wire and attach at the back/top of the wreath for hanging.

String-Me-Along Cards

Gather friends and family together to make these creative dimensional cards. These special greetings will be kept as a treasured piece of art worthy to be the center of attention on the mantel or hung on the Christmas tree.

Here's What You Need

Assortment of card-weight textured papers (available at crafts, discount, or office stores)
Straight and decorative-edge scissors
Pencil; thick white crafts glue
Assortment of cords, string of beads
White acrylic paint
Paintbrush
Water
Pearl acrylic paints in lime green, orange, and pink
Gold rubbing medium such as gold Rub 'n Buff
Gold beads for accents

Here's What You Do

Cut the paper to any size and shape you wish. There are many textures of papers you can purchase. You may want to cut the paper to fit a standard envelope.

With a pencil, draw the design you wish to create. Using the patterns, *right,* as inspiration, make fluid, irregular shaped hearts, a zig-zag tree, or spell out a holiday word. Outline the pencil path with crafts glue. Lay down a piece of thick cord, braid, or tiny string of beads along the glue path. Allow to dry. Paint the entire piece with several coats of white acrylic paint. Allow to dry.

Paint each card a color of your choice. We used pearlized pastel pink, orange, and green. Let dry.

Using a very small amount of gold Rub 'n Buff applied to your finger, gently rub over raised surfaces, highlighting those areas. Embellish with glued gold beads.

Layer other papers under the decorated card (as for the Joy card) or add papers on top as we did with the star on the tree card.

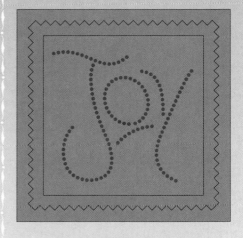

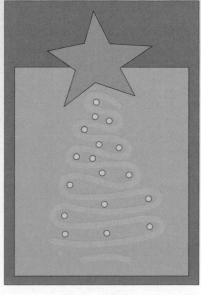

Everyone that comes to visit will be charmed by this cross-stitch piece created by you. Stitched on Aida cloth, the piece works up quickly and is embellished with golden buttons and jingle bells.

Welcome Cross-stitch

HERE'S WHAT YOU NEED

*12×6-inch piece of 16-count white
  Aida cloth*

*Cotton embroidery floss in colors listed
  in key*

Kreinik gold #8 braid

Needle; embroidery hoop

*Three gold star buttons with holes in
  the front*

3×10¹/₂-inch piece of matboard

2 small jingle bells

¹/₄ yard of fleece

Thick white crafts glue

3×10¹/₂-inch piece of white felt

4-inch piece of ¹/₈ inch dowel

1 yard of fine gold braid

2 star buttons with holes in the sides

¹/₄ yard of thin red ribbon

HERE'S WHAT YOU DO

Find center of the chart and the center of the fabric; begin stitching there. Use two plies of floss for all cross-stitches. Work the

backstitches using one ply of floss or braid. Press piece on back side. Sew star button with holes in front at ×'s near M. Sew small jingle bell at × near W.

To mount, cut the end of the matboard to a point. Lay stitchery over board and trim 1 inch all around. Cut fleece and felt to fit board and glue fleece to board front. Wrap stitchery around fleece and board and glue on back securing dowel at the top under stitchery. Glue felt to back. Glue braiding around edge. Tie ribbon at corners of dowel and glue star buttons, with holes in sides, to ends. Sew jingle bell to the bottom point.

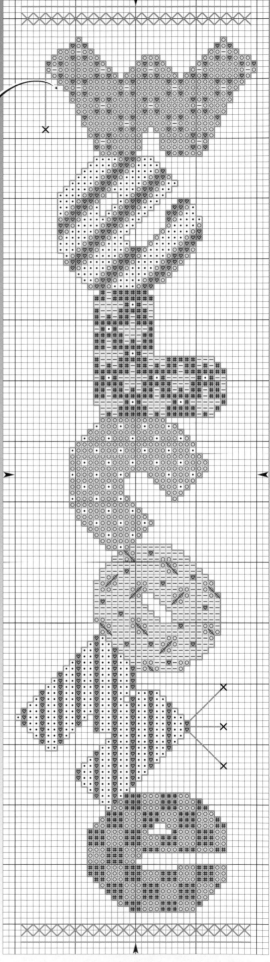

Anchor		DMC
002	·	000 White
9046	♥	321 Christmas red
297	–	444 Lemon
239	O	702 Christmas green
132	#	797 Royal blue

BACKSTITCH (1X)

381	/	938 Coffee brown – leaf veins in letter "O"
	/	002 Kreinik Gold #8 braid – all other stitches

Stitch count: 155 high x 40 wide

Finished design sizes:
14-count fabric – 11 x 2⁷/₈ inches
16-count fabric – 9⁵/₈ x 2¹/₂ inches
18-count fabric – 8⁵/₈ x 2¹/₄ inches

More Ways to
Greet

We all want to greet our family and friends in a way that makes them feel comfortable. Here are some quick ideas for making your guests feel at home.

For an elegant outdoor display, place votive candles in holiday colors in sand-filled canning jars. Just before holiday guests arrive, light the luminarias for a warm and festive greeting.

To display the holiday greeting cards you receive, use a paper punch to make a hole in a corner and use ribbon to attach the cards to holiday greenery atop a mantel or down an indoor railing.

Make your guests departure as warm as their arrival by giving them a few fresh-baked cookies in cellophane tied with a bow. They can enjoy your gift from the kitchen on their drive home.

Search flea markets for small chairs or stools that can be placed outside at the front door. Place a wreath or other arrangement on the chair for a warm welcome.

🍃 Make room in your home for visitors to place their outerwear. Clean out the closet and have plenty of hangers on hand. Also get a boot tray to catch any drips off shoes or boots.

🍃 A quick way to dress up outdoor lights is by tying matching ribbon bows to each of the fixtures. You can also place a bow on the mailbox.

🍃 For a sparkling greeting, be sure to clean all window and door glass before putting up holiday lights. The reflections will be much merrier.

🍃 If the weather allows, give children sidewalk chalk and have them draw welcoming holiday messages on the driveway.

🍃 When children are coming to visit, you may want to hire one of Santa's helpers or rent a Santa suit for the occasion. Imagine their expressions if St. Nick himself greeted them at the door.

🍃 When you open your door to holiday guests, have Christmas music softly playing in the background. The familiar tunes will set a festive mood.

🍃 When mailing holiday cards, choose holiday stickers or sealing wax to place on the back of the envelopes for an extra special touch.

Decorate

Remember

Nourish

Light

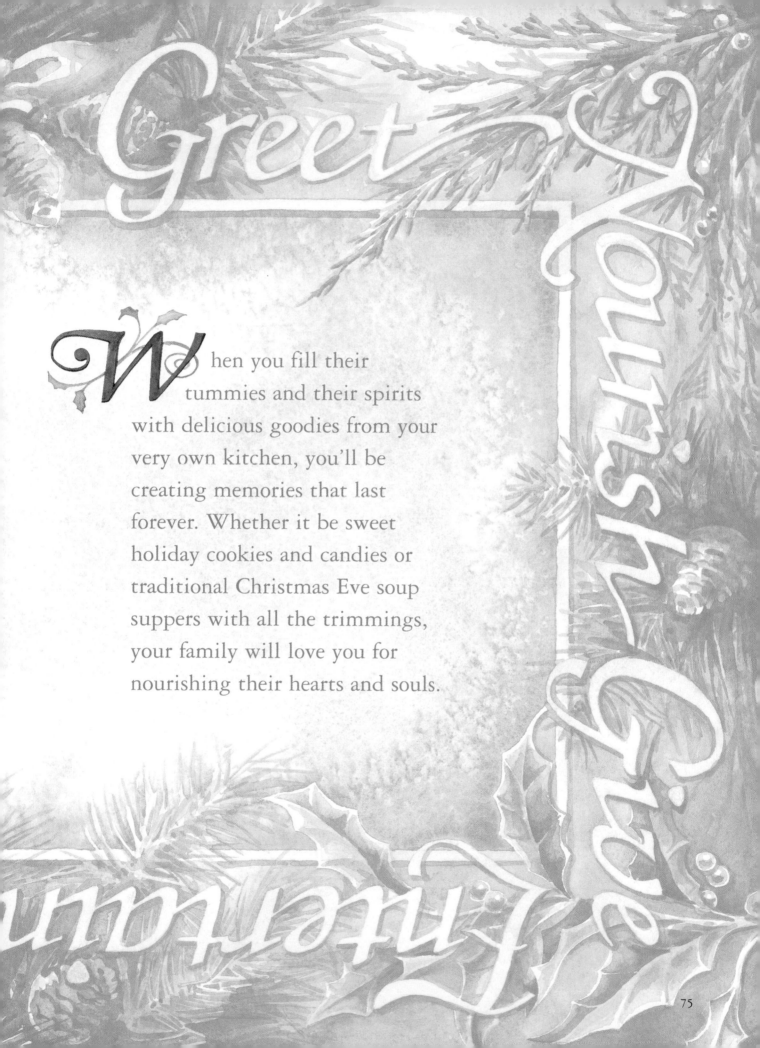

When you fill their tummies and their spirits with delicious goodies from your very own kitchen, you'll be creating memories that last forever. Whether it be sweet holiday cookies and candies or traditional Christmas Eve soup suppers with all the trimmings, your family will love you for nourishing their hearts and souls.

HOLIDAY SWEETS

Christmas is a time to show your creative talents in the kitchen by making sweet goodies that become asked-for-favorites every year.

This collection of sweet-tooth recipes offers some traditional favorites with a new twist and some pretty ideas that look so fancy but take very little time.

Sweet Popcorn Treats

Popcorn balls have long been a holiday favorite. Their sticky candy coating compliments the salty, buttery popcorn in a way that no other goodie can. We gave ours a candy cane handle, wrapped them in plastic wrap, and tied them with a jingle bell bow. Keep a basket by the door for a treat for anyone that comes to call. The recipe is on *page 85*.

Heavenly Divinity

As light and smooth as can be, this traditional favorite is always the first to disappear from the holiday candy plate. We've added a touch of peppermint candy to make this recipe just a little sweeter. The recipe is on *page 85*.

Designed to resemble colorful fruit marzipan, these easy-to-make candies will be the talk of the table. Package them as elegant gifts or present them arranged on the holiday candy tray. The recipe is on *page 85*.

Sugared Candy Fruits

Honeycomb Toffee Brittle

Light and crunchy, this melt-in-your mouth candy will remind you of toffee and brittle at the same time. So quick to make, this candy only uses five ingredients. The recipe is on *page 86.*

Grandma's Favorite Cookies

Your holiday cookie tray isn't complete without *Grandma's Sugar Cookies*. Try a coating of chocolate or butterscotch for a simple new twist. Serve *Praline Cookies* with hot chocolate or a coffee latte. Recipes for both cookies are on *page 86*.

Country Shortbread Cookies

These deliciously rich cookies have been made for generations using only three ingredients. Always mixed by hand, they were decorated with a simple stamped design made from a favorite button. The recipe is on *page* 87.

Holiday Chocolate Cake

What fun to have a red chocolate cake to match the holiday fun. This cake gets its rich color and moist texture from rich red beets. We frosted ours with a white-as-snow icing and used Santa as the center of attention. The recipe is on *page 87*.

Peppermint Angel Dessert

This pretty dessert combines angel food cake and whipped cream and is a delight to make. Be sure to add the tiny holiday touches of shaved chocolate curls. The recipe is on *page 87.*

Sweet Popcorn Treats

Sticky and sweet, popcorn balls are always a favorite. Wrap up extras for sweet gifts.

HERE'S WHAT YOU NEED
1	Cup unpopped corn (popped)
2	Cups granulated sugar
1 1/2	Cups water
1/2	Teaspoon salt
1/2	Cup light corn syrup
1	Teaspoon butter
1	Teaspoon vinegar
1	Teaspoon vanilla
1/2	Teaspoon baking soda
1/4	Teaspoon cream of tartar

HERE'S WHAT YOU DO
Pop corn. Remove all unpopped kernels. Place in large cake pan or roasting pan and keep warm in a 225°F oven.

Combine the sugar, water, salt, corn syrup, butter, and vinegar. Cook to hard ball stage (250°F on a candy thermometer). Stir in the vanilla, baking soda, and cream of tartar. Mix well. Remove the popcorn from the oven and pour the syrup mixture over the corn. Mix well. Butter your hands to easily shape popcorn into balls. Insert a candy cane into center of ball. Cool. Wrap with plastic wrap and tie with a ribbon. Tie a jingle bell at the end of the ribbon. Makes about 18 balls.

Heavenly Divinity

Add sky-blue peppermint pieces to make this holiday favorite extra special.

HERE'S WHAT YOU NEED
2 1/2	Cups sugar
3/4	Cup white syrup
1/4	Cup hot water
2	Egg whites
	Candy cane pieces, cherries, or chopped nuts

HERE'S WHAT YOU DO
Mix together the sugar, white syrup, and hot water; set aside. Beat the egg whites until soft peaks form.

Bring the sugar mixture to a boil and boil until thread stage or 248°F on a candy thermometer. Pour the mixture slowly into the egg whites continuing to beat the egg whites on high speed while adding the syrup mixture. Beat until the mixture forms stiff peaks.

Drop by spoonfuls onto a greased cookie sheet. Top with bits of candy canes, cherries, or chopped nuts. Makes about 3 dozen pieces.

Sugared Candy Fruits

Who would believe that these elegant candies are so easy to make. Colored gelatin, is the secret to these sweet treats.

HERE'S WHAT YOU NEED
(FOR EACH COLOR OF FRUIT)
1	3 ounce package flavored gelatin in color and flavor to best match each fruit. For lemons or pears, use lemon (yellow) gelatin. For apples, use red (cherry) gelatin.
1/2	Cup pecans, finely ground
1/2	Cup flaked coconut
1/3	Cup plus 1 tablespoon sweetened condensed milk
1/2	Teaspoon vanilla
	Food coloring and decorative sugar appropriate for fruit
	Toothpicks (to shape fruit)
	Green gumdrops (for leaves)
	Whole cloves (for stems)

HERE'S WHAT YOU DO
Combine the gelatin, ground pecans, coconut, condensed milk, and vanilla. Mix well. Chill for at least 1 hour.

We made apples, peaches, pears, limes, lemons, and plums. Start with a small ball of dough the size of a quarter. Roll in decorative

continued on page 86

sugar for the color appropriate for the particular fruit color. To make the green leaves, roll a green gumdrop between two pieces of waxed paper. Use a knife to shape the leaves. For the apple, make the top bigger than the bottom. Put a whole clove in for the stem and add a gumdrop leaf. For the peach, use a toothpick to make a line down the side. Add a stem and leaf. For the pear, make the top smaller than the bottom and add a gumdrop leaf and stem. For the limes and lemon, point the ends. For the plum, make into an oval and make a line down the side. Each recipe makes about 12 fruits.

Honeycomb Toffee Brittle

This delightful candy combines the delicate texture of a nut brittle with the richness of a sweet toffee.

HERE'S WHAT YOU NEED

1	Cup sugar
1	Cup white syrup
1	Tablespoon baking soda
1	Cup semi-sweet chocolate chips
1/2	Cup walnuts, chopped

HERE'S WHAT YOU DO

Grease a cookie sheet with butter. Set aside. Combine sugar and syrup in a medium saucepan. Bring to a boil over medium heat without stirring until the mixture reaches 280°F on a candy thermometer. (This takes about 20 minutes.) Remove from heat, stir down. Return to heat and continue to cook until it reaches 295°F on a candy thermometer. Remove from heat and stir in baking soda. The syrup will foam up. Stir quickly and pour onto the cookie sheet. Melt chocolate chips in double boiler and drizzle over brittle. Sprinkle with chopped nuts. When candy is completely cooled, break into pieces. Makes about 1 1/2 pounds.

Praline Cookies

Sweet and rich, these pecan cookies are close cousins to praline candy.

HERE'S WHAT YOU NEED

1/2	Cup butter
1 1/2	Cups brown sugar
1	Large egg
1	Teaspoon vanilla
1 2/3	Cups all-purpose flour
1 1/2	Teaspoons baking powder
1/2	Teaspoon salt
1	Recipe Pecan Frosting

HERE'S WHAT YOU DO

Cream the butter, brown sugar, egg, and vanilla. Sift the dry ingredients together and add to the creamed mixture. Drop dough by teaspoonfuls on a greased cookie sheet. Bake at 350°F for 10 to 12 minutes.

For the *Pecan Frosting*, mix 1/2 cup *heavy cream* and 1 cup *brown sugar*. Boil for 1 minute and add 1 cup *powdered sugar* and 1 cup *chopped pecans*. Cool slightly. Frost cookies. Makes 3 dozen cookies.

Grandma's Sugar Cookies

Not too sweet, this family sugar cookie recipe loves to be frosted or dipped in chocolate.

HERE'S WHAT YOU NEED

2	Cups sugar
1	Cup butter
3	Eggs
1	Teaspoon salt
1	Teaspoon vanilla
5 1/2	Cups sifted flour
1	Teaspoon soda
1	Teaspoon baking powder
1/3	Cup milk

HERE'S WHAT YOU DO

Cream the sugar, butter, and eggs. Add the salt and vanilla. Sift the dry ingredients together; add alternately with the milk. Batter will be sticky. Cover dough. Refrigerate for 3 hours or overnight. Roll out on lightly floured board to desired thickness, about 1/4-inch-thick. Cut out with cookie cutters. Bake at 360°F for about 10 minutes.

Melt 2 cups *chocolate* or *butterscotch chips* in a double boiler. Dip cookie into chocolate. Place on waxed paper to harden. Makes about 4 dozen cookies.

Country Shortbread Cookies

Three ingredients are all that's needed to make these rich shortbreads.

HERE'S WHAT YOU NEED

1	Cup butter, softened
1/2	Cup plus 2 tablespoons sugar
2 1/2	Cups all-purpose flour

HERE'S WHAT YOU DO

Mix the butter and sugar with your hands. Stir in the flour. Make into a ball and chill for 15 minutes. Roll out to 1/3-inch thickness. Cut into 2-inch circles or any other desired shape. To make a design in the dough press a fancy button into it so a slight impression forms. Bake at 325°F for 12 minutes. Makes 24 small cookies.

Holiday Chocolate Cake

Beautiful red beets give this cake its glorious holiday color and moist texture.

HERE'S WHAT YOU NEED

1 1/2	Cups drained canned beets
3	Eggs
1 1/2	Cups sugar
1	Cup oil
2	Tablespoons butter
1/2	Cup cocoa
1 3/4	Cups all-purpose flour
1 1/2	Teaspoons baking soda
1/4	Teaspoon baking powder
1/2	Teaspoon salt
2	Teaspoons vanilla
3	Teaspoons red food coloring
1	Recipe White Frosting

HERE'S WHAT YOU DO

Puree drained beets using a blender. Combine all ingredients in large bowl. Mix well, and pour into a greased bundt pan or 9×13-inch cake pan. Bake at 350°F until toothpick inserted in center comes out clean (50 minutes for bundt pan and 35 minutes for cake pan).

For *White Frosting*, combine 2 1/2 cups *powdered sugar*, 3 1/2 tablespoons *milk*, 1 1/2 tablespoons *shortening*, 1 tablespoon *corn syrup*, 1 teaspoon *vanilla*, 1 teaspoon *butter flavoring*, and 1/2 teaspoon *almond extract*. Frost cake.

Peppermint Angel Dessert

Chocolate and peppermint combine to give this dessert its heavenly taste.

HERE'S WHAT YOU NEED

1	Chocolate angel food cake
1	Cup half-and-half cream
1	Pound peppermint sticks, crushed (about 1 1/2 cups)
2	Envelopes unflavored gelatin
1 1/2	Cups heavy cream
1	8-oz. container whipped topping
1	Recipe Shadow Frosting

HERE'S WHAT YOU DO

Tear cake into medium size pieces. Place loosely in a 13×9-inch baking dish. Heat half-and-half in a double boiler; add the crushed peppermint candy. Heat until candy dissolves. Add gelatin which has been softened in 4 tablespoons cold water. Cool. Whip heavy cream and fold into mixture. Pour over and mix with the cake pieces. (This must be done before candy mixture sets.) Chill until set. Frost with whipped topping. Drizzle Shadow Frosting mixture on top. Garnish with chocolate curls.

For the *Shadow Frosting* melt 1 square *baking chocolate* with 1/2 tablespoon *butter*. Drizzle over topping. Drag knife lightly over the top creating a zigzag effect.

CHRISTMAS EVE

A time for quiet family gatherings and genuine celebration, Christmas Eve should be a night of simple pleasures. That means easy-to-make recipes for you to prepare for your family on that special night.

With all the wonderful excitement that the night before Christmas brings—whether you're coming in from caroling, getting ready for the children's program at church, or finishing that last handmade gift, you'll want nutritious and comforting food to present to your family.

Come in from the winter cold and be welcomed by this steaming cup of *Hearty Minestrone Soup*. A favorite Christmas carol and *Sesame Breadsticks* make the Christmas Eve supper complete. The recipes are on *page 93*.

Hearty Minestrone Soup

Tiny Treats

Your family will love to sample these *Smoky Wrap Ups*, *Bubbly Cheese Squares*, and *Mini Pasta Flowerettes* as they enjoy the holiday spirit that fills your kitchen on Christmas Eve. All the recipes are on *pages 93–94.*

Old-Fashioned Chicken and Noodles

Thick and rich and full of flavor, this old time dish will become one that is asked for every year. Let the children help make the noodles. It will be a time to visit about the exciting day ahead. The recipe is on *page 95*.

Cran-Apple Bars

Cranberries and apples make a delightfully sweet combination for these holiday cookies. The crust is a simple butter and sugar based pastry that turns into a visual beauty when cut and woven on top. The recipe is on *page 95*.

Hearty Minestrone Soup

Bow-tie pasta makes this oh-so-nutritious soup even more appealing for the holidays.

HERE'S WHAT YOU NEED

1	Tablespoon olive oil
1	Small onion
1/4	Cup celery, diced
1/4	Cup red bell pepper, chopped
1/4	Cup green bell pepper, chopped
1/8	Teaspoon **each** of oregano, basil, garlic, and pepper
1/2	Teaspoon of dried parsley
1	Teaspoon salt
1	Can beef broth (14.5oz)
1	Can chicken broth (14.5oz)
1/2	Cup fresh broccoli flowerettes
1/2	Cup fresh green beans, cut up
1/2	Cup carrots, sliced
1	Can diced tomatoes (14.5oz)
1	Cup uncooked bow-tie macaroni
	Parmesan cheese, shredded

HERE'S WHAT YOU DO

Saute onion, celery, and peppers in oil. Add spices, salt, and pepper. Add beef and chicken broth. Let simmer 10 minutes. Steam broccoli, beans, and carrots until tender. Add vegetables and canned tomatoes to broth. Add macaroni to the broth mixture. Cook until macaroni becomes tender. Serve with shredded parmesan cheese. Makes 6 servings.

Sesame Breadsticks

Perfect to serve with winter's hot soups and stews, these pretty breadsticks are soft and buttery.

HERE'S WHAT YOU NEED

1	Package rapid rise yeast
1/2	Tablespoon sugar
1/4	Cup warm water
1/2	Cup warm water
1	Tablespoon sugar
1	Teaspoon salt
2	Tablespoons olive oil
1	Egg yolk
2 1/4	Cups all-purpose flour
1	Egg white
1	Tablespoon water
	Sesame seeds

HERE'S WHAT YOU DO

Dissolve yeast and 1/2 tablespoon sugar in 1/4 cup warm water. Add the 1/2 cup warm water, 1 tablespoon sugar, salt, olive oil, and egg yolk. Add the flour gradually to this mixture.

Beat with mixer on low until mixed and then on high for 3 minutes. Knead dough until smooth. Cover and let rise for 1 hour. Punch down and divide into 16 pieces. Roll each piece into an 8-inch rope. Twist and place on a greased cookie sheet 2 inches apart. Let rise for 45 minutes. Before baking, beat 1 egg white and 1 tablespoon water. Brush over breadsticks and sprinkle with sesame seeds.

Bake at 425°F for 10 minutes or until golden brown. Makes sixteen 8-inch breadsticks.

Mini Pasta Flowerettes

Presented as tiny flower petals on an appetizer tray, these pasta-filled tomatoes are always a favorite alone or to accompany a light evening meal.

HERE'S WHAT YOU NEED

1	Cup acini-di-pepe pasta, cooked and drained
2	Tablespoons finely diced green, red, and yellow peppers
3	Tablespoons finely diced black and green olives
1	Tablespoon finely chopped celery
1/2	Teaspoon salt
1/2	Tablespoon pepper
3	Tablespoons Italian salad dressing
	About eleven large cherry or small Roma tomatoes
	Yellow bell pepper cut into fine strips

continued on page 94

HERE'S WHAT YOU DO

Cook the pasta according to package instructions and drain well. Add the finely diced peppers, finely diced olives, and chopped celery. Add the salt and pepper to taste. Stir in the Italian dressing and mix well. Cover and chill.

Slice the tomatoes in half and scoop out the inside using a spoon. Carefully stuff the tomatoes with the pasta mixture.

Arrange three halves of the cherry tomatoes together with the small ends toward the middle creating the illusion of a flower. Place three yellow pepper strips vertically in the middle of each group of three tomatoes resembling stamens for the flower. Makes about 21 small tomatoes or 7 flowerettes.

Smoky Wrap Ups

Tiny cocktail wieners are always a favorite at holiday time. Instead of serving them in a sauce this year, dress them up with a simple piecrust dough to make them even more special for holiday entertaining.

HERE'S WHAT YOU NEED

3	Cups all-purpose flour
1/2	Teaspoon salt
1	Cup butter flavored shortening
1	Egg
5	Teaspoons cold water
1	Teaspoon vinegar
1	Package cocktail wieners

HERE'S WHAT YOU DO

Mix the flour and salt together. Cut in the shortening. Set aside. Mix the egg, water, and vinegar together and add to the flour mixture. Do not overmix. Roll out the dough as for piecrust (about 1/4-inch thick). Cut into 4-inch squares. Place cocktail wiener on the square diagonally. Fold over the corners of the dough. Place on a greased cookie sheet. Bake at 400°F for about 10 to 12 minutes or until golden brown. Makes about 24 servings.

Bubbly Cheese Squares

So easy to make, these yummy bite-size treats will be requested every year. Make plenty and freeze them to have on hand when friends come to call.

HERE'S WHAT YOU NEED

1 1/2	Pounds ground chuck
1/2	Pound Italian sausage
1	Pound processed cheese
1/2	Teaspoon oregano powder
1	Teaspoon Worcestershire sauce
1	Package party rye bread

HERE'S WHAT YOU DO

Brown the ground beef and the sausage. Drain well. Cube the cheese and mix with the drained meat. Melt over stove, stirring constantly, or melt in microwave stirring as necessary until completely melted.

Mix in the oregano and Worcestershire sauce. Spread mixture on the rye bread slices mounding the meat and cheese on each piece. Place under the broiler until bubbly, about 5 minutes. Serve immediately. Makes about 24 individual pieces. To freeze, cover with foil and place in freezer. Thaw in refrigerator before broiling. Do not refreeze.

Old-Fashioned Chicken and Noodles

A favorite for generations, this comfort food is a perfect choice for Christmas Eve. For a hearty meal, serve over mashed potatoes or baking powder biscuits.

HERE'S WHAT YOU NEED

1	Whole chicken
	Water to cover chicken
1	Teaspoon salt
1/2	Cup celery, chopped
1	Small onion

For the noodles:

2	Cups all-purpose flour
1	Teaspoon salt
1	Egg
3	Egg yolks
1/4–1/2	Cup water

HERE'S WHAT YOU DO

Wash the chicken and cut up into pieces. Place in large pan on stove and cover with water. Add salt, celery, and onion, and cook until tender, about 30 minutes. Remove the chicken from the bone, cut up, cover, and set aside in refrigerator. Strain broth and set aside.

To make the noodles, mix the flour and salt and place in a large bowl. Set aside. Beat the egg and add the egg yolks and water, mixing well. With a spoon make a well in the center of the dry ingredients. Add the eggs and water mixture. Mix until it forms a ball and knead until smooth.

Dust the rolling surface with flour. With a rolling pin, roll the dough into a rectangle about 1/4-inch thick. Cut into 1/8-inch strips for narrow noodles or 1/4-inch strips for wider noodles. Shake noodles out after cutting and place on a floured cookie sheet. Set aside.

Bring the broth to a boil in a crock pot or large pan. Add the noodles; cook until tender, about 4 hours in crock pot on high or about 20 minutes on the stove. Add the cut up chicken. Makes about 8 servings.

Cran-Apple Bars

Made with cranberries and apples and adorned with rich pie pastry, these colorful bars will steal the show. These bars freeze beautifully, so make them ahead of time and present them on Christmas Eve.

HERE'S WHAT YOU NEED

2	Cups all-purpose flour
1/2	Cup sugar
1/2	Teaspoon vanilla
2	Egg yolks
1	Cup butter, softened
2	Cups cranberries, frozen
1	Granny Smith apple, finely diced
2	Tablespoons orange juice concentrate
1 1/2	Cups sugar
2	Tablespoons cornstarch
1/8	Teaspoon ginger
1/2	Teaspoon salt
1/2	Cup chopped nuts

HERE'S WHAT YOU DO

For the pastry, mix the flour, 1/2 cup sugar, vanilla, and egg yolks. Cut the butter into this mixture. Form into a ball and chill for 1 hour.

Grind the frozen cranberries. Mix the cranberries, and apples with the orange juice, 1 1/2 cups sugar, cornstarch, ginger, and salt. Simmer on the stove until thick (about 15 minutes). Add the chopped nuts. Chill.

Press 2/3 of the pastry into a 9×13-inch pan. Spread with cranberry apple filling. Roll out the remaining pastry to about a 1/4-inch thickness. Cut into narrow (about 1/2-inch-wide) strips using a pastry wheel. Arrange the strips in criss cross fashion across the top of the filling. Bake at 375°F for about 20 minutes. Cool and cut into squares or narrow rectangles. Makes about 3 dozen small bars.

When the big morning finally arrives, you'll be all smiles with your breakfast menu planned well in advance. Everyone will want to see what Santa has brought for them and then they'll be hungry for a special Christmas

Yummy Frosted Orange Rolls

Grated orange rind is the secret to these delicious sweet rolls drizzled with orange juice frosting. Make each roll just a little larger than usual for the big day and the smiles will last all day long. For a quick Christmas morning gift for a favorite neighbor, place the roll on a small plate and wrap with a piece of clear cellophane and a pretty red bow. The recipe is on *page 102.*

morning breakfast. The excitement will continue when you present your family with delicious treats you made especially for them. Your secret is that you made them weeks ago and kept them for the big day.

Breakfast Sausage Roll

Filled with hearty sausage, mushrooms, and cheese, this make-ahead treat is a breakfast rolled up all in one. Made with frozen bread, you'll want to have plenty on hand. The recipe is on *pages 102–103*.

They'll ask for more when they taste these oh-so-light rolls filled with cinnamon and sugar and covered with caramel and pecans. The rolls can be made ahead, frozen, and warmed up quickly. The recipe is on *page 102*.

Caramel Pecan Pull-Aparts

Ready to slice on Christmas morning, this pumpkin bread is full of sugar and spice. Make extra to freeze and serve or give to friends that come to wish you a Merry Christmas. The recipe is on *page 103.*

Pumpkin Loaves

Favorite Fruitcake

Here's a delightful fruitcake that everyone will love. These beautiful cakes can be made weeks in advance and frozen to have ready for Christmas morning. Try baking them in a round can or star-shaped tin for a festive look. The recipe is on *page 103*.

Frosted Orange Rolls

As yummy to look at as they are to eat, these sweet rolls will bring happy smiles on Christmas morning.

HERE'S WHAT YOU NEED

1/3	Cup sugar
1	Teaspoon salt
1/3	Cup butter
1	Cup scalded milk
1	Package of dry yeast
1/4	Cup warm water
1	Egg, beaten
3	Tablespoons grated orange rind
4	Cups all-purpose flour
1	Recipe Orange Frosting

HERE'S WHAT YOU DO

Place sugar, salt, and butter in pan. Add milk. Heat and stir until butter is melted. Dissolve yeast in the warm water in a 2-quart bowl. Add cooled milk mixture, beaten egg, and orange rind. Add flour to form a stiff dough. Turn out and knead until smooth and elastic, about 5 minutes, using more flour if necessary. Place in bowl; let rise until doubled. Punch down and

roll into a 9×13-inch rectangle. Spread with 1/4 cup *butter*, 1/4 cup *sugar*, 1 teaspoon *cinnamon*. Roll up and slice into 1 1/2-inch slices. Place in greased muffin tin. Let rise for 45 minutes. Bake at 350°F for 20 minutes or until brown. Cool. Drizzle with Orange Frosting. Makes 16 rolls. Can be frozen for up to 3 weeks.

For **Orange Frosting**, mix 1 tablespoon *butter*, 1 cup *powdered sugar*, 2 tablespoons *orange juice*.

Caramel-Pecan Pull Aparts

The secret is dry milk in these oh-so-light pecan rolls.

HERE'S WHAT YOU NEED

1/2	Cup milk
1	Cup lukewarm water
1/2	Cup dry milk
2	Packages dry yeast
1	Tablespoon sugar
3/4	Cup shortening
3/4	Cup sugar
2	Teaspoons salt
2	Eggs, beaten
6–7	Cups all-purpose flour
1	Cup pecan halves

HERE'S WHAT YOU DO

Mix the milk, water, dry milk, yeast, and 1 tablespoon sugar together in a bowl. Set aside. Melt

the shortening. Allow to cool. Add the 3/4 cup sugar, shortening, salt, and beaten eggs to the yeast mixture. Beat in the flour until it is stiff. Turn out on floured board and knead until smooth and elastic. Set in large bowl and cover with damp towel and let rise for about an hour. Punch down and roll half of the dough out into a 9×13-inch rectangle shape. Spread with 1/4 cup *butter*, 1/4 cup *brown sugar*, 1/4 cup *white sugar*, and 1 teaspoon *cinnamon*. Roll up and slice into 1 1/2-inch slices.

In the bottom of an 8×8-inch pan, mix 1/4 cup melted *butter*, 1/4 cup *brown sugar*, and 1 teaspoon *white syrup*. Lay pecans upside down in butter mixture. Lay the rolls in pan over the mixture. Repeat for other half of dough. Bake at 350°F for about 25 minutes. Turn upside down on foil. Makes 18 rolls.

Breakfast Sausage Roll

Sliced and served with fruit or juice, this delicious roll is a breakfast all in one.

HERE'S WHAT YOU NEED

2	Loaves purchased frozen bread
1	Pound Italian sausage
1	Pound hamburger
1	Cup broccoli, chopped
1 1/2	Cups mozzarella cheese, shredded
1/2	Cup mushroom, sliced

HERE'S WHAT YOU DO

Thaw bread and roll out each loaf to a 9×11-inch rectangle. Brown meat and drain. Add broccoli, cheese, and mushrooms. Spread half of the mixture on each rolled out rectangle. Roll up from the long side and seal the edges by pinching them together. Place each loaf on a greased cookie sheet and let rise about 1 hour. Bake at 325°F for about 35 minutes. Each loaf makes about 6 servings. To freeze, place on greased cookie sheet, cover and freeze immediately. When ready to bake, thaw in refrigerator overnight. Bake as directed above.

Pumpkin Loaves

So moist and full of flavor and so very quick to make, bake an extra batch for great hostess gifts.

HERE'S WHAT YOU NEED

3 1/3	Cups all-purpose flour
3	Cups sugar
2	Teaspoons baking soda
1 1/2	Teaspoons salt
1	Teaspoon nutmeg
1	Teaspoon cinnamon
1/4	Teaspoon cloves
1	Cup vegetable oil
4	Eggs
2/3	Cup water
2	Cups canned pumpkin
1	Recipe Frosting Glaze

HERE'S WHAT YOU DO

Sift all dry ingredients together. Add the oil, eggs, water, and pumpkin to the dry ingredients. Mix well and pour into 3 large greased bread pans. Bake at 350°F for 1 hour. Cool. Makes 3 loaves.

For *Frosting Glaze*, mix 1 cup *powdered sugar*, 1 teaspoon *green food coloring*, and 1 tablespoon *milk*. Drizzle loaves with frosting. Garnish with candied cherries. Wrap in foil to freeze.

Favorite Fruitcake

Here's a fruitcake you'll love to slice and serve with that first morning cup of coffee. The magic ingredients in this fruitcake are grape jelly and lots of candied fruits and nuts.

HERE'S WHAT YOU NEED

1	Cup butter
1	Cup sugar
5	Eggs
1	Cup grape jelly
1/2	Cup orange juice
2 1/2	Cups flour
1	Teaspoon baking powder
1	Teaspoon cinnamon
1/2	Teaspoon **each** nutmeg, allspice, cloves, and salt
1	Cup candied whole cherries
1	Cup blanched unsalted almonds
1	Cup pecans
1	Cup white raisins
1	Cup raisins
1/2	Cup candied pineapple
1/4	Cup candied orange peel
1/4	Cup chopped dates
1/2	Cup coconut
1/2	Cup dried apricots

HERE'S WHAT YOU DO

Cream together the butter, sugar, eggs, and grape jelly. Sift and add the dry ingredients alternately with the orange juice. Mix well. Set aside.

In a large bowl mix the dried and candied fruits, nuts, and coconut. Do not cut or chop the nuts too finely. Add the 1/2 cup flour to this mixture and stir together. Add to the batter.

To prepare the pans, grease with margarine or cooking spray. Line with waxed paper or cooking parchment. Spray or grease the paper again. Pour the batter into pans. Do not smooth the top. Bake at 300°F for about 1 hour or until toothpick comes out clean. Invert onto foil covered rack. Wait 24 hours before slicing. If you want a round cake, grease a clean vegetable can and line the bottom with waxed paper or parchment. Invert pans on rack to cool. Makes 3 standard bread pans or 6 small round pans.

More Ways to Nourish

There's no better place than the kitchen to gather and share the holiday fun. Here are some quick ways to nourish your family during holiday time that start in the kitchen.

❧ Surprise the kids on Christmas morning with holiday toast. Use large cookie cutters to cut shapes such as stars, bells, and stockings. Spread honey or jellies on the toast shapes to complete the fun.

❧ Plain vanilla ice cream becomes a special holiday treat when sprinkled with green and red candies found in the baking section of the grocery store.

❧ Before doing your holiday grocery shopping, ask each member of the family to choose a favorite recipe to make during the holidays. Be sure to include the ingredients on your shopping list.

❧ To spend as much time as possible with family and friends during the holidays, do your baking ahead of time. Select recipes in which the baked goods can be made and frozen.

🍃 If your family loves decorated sugar cookies, let them join in the fun. You bake the cookies in a variety of shapes, supply the frosting and decorations, and let dad and the kids do the rest.

🍃 When doing your holiday shopping, stock up on toss-away food containers. They will come in handy when you want to send goodies home with your guests.

🍃 During the holidays, remember to keep healthy snacks on hand. Carrots, celery, and other bite-size veggies make a great last-minute snack.

🍃 For an easy holiday dessert, mix up red flavored gelatin. Let set until slightly thickened. Fold in a small container of whipped dairy topping. Refrigerate until set.

🍃 Add a taste of peppermint to holiday desserts by crushing up candy canes. Sprinkle over frosted brownies, cake, or vanilla ice cream.

🍃 Remember to nourish your outdoor friends by supplying birds, squirrels, or other visitors with the appropriate foods.

🍃 Buy some pretty baskets to have on hand. Fill them with colored tissue, and then add canned vegetables, fruits, sauces, or pastas to give as last-minute gifts.

Decorate

Remember

Give

Light

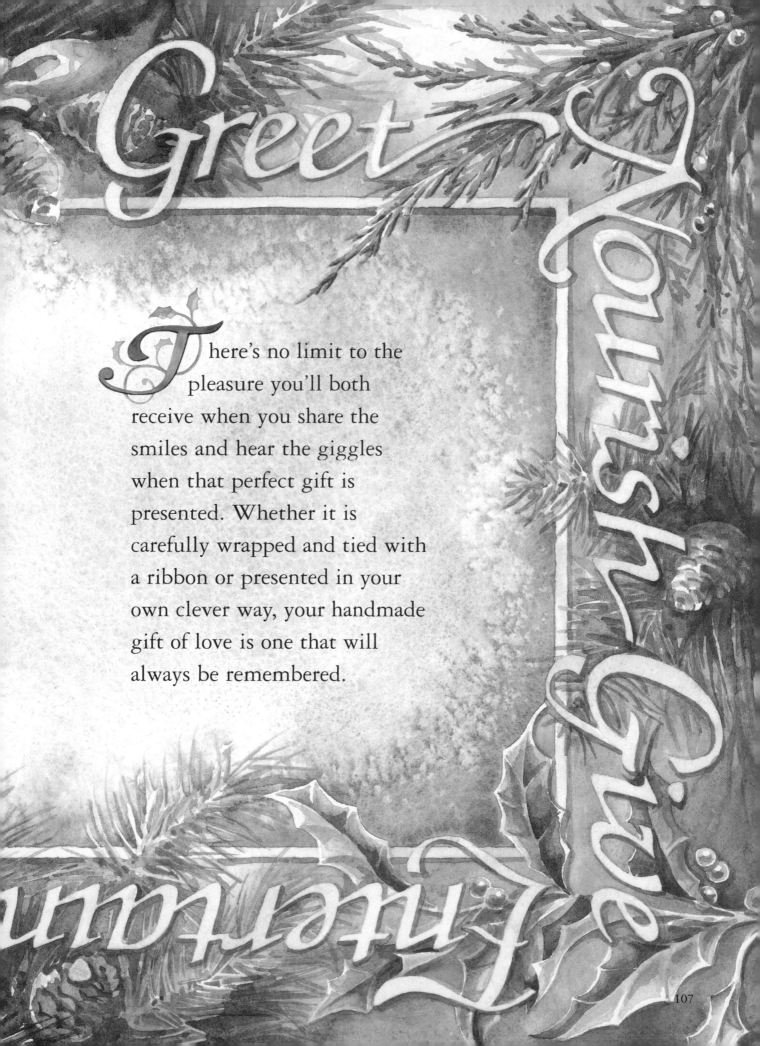

There's no limit to the pleasure you'll both receive when you share the smiles and hear the giggles when that perfect gift is presented. Whether it is carefully wrapped and tied with a ribbon or presented in your own clever way, your handmade gift of love is one that will always be remembered.

Floss Flower Pot

Wrapped up for Christmas with bright embroidery floss and embellished with a tassel trim, this gift of flowers will need no other wrap. Choose from a variety of beautiful floss colors to match any decorating scheme.

HERE'S WHAT YOU NEED

5-inch terra cotta flower pot
White crafts glue
About 5 skeins of embroidery floss in reds and greens
Purchased red tassel
1 yard of decorator braid (available in the upholstery section of the fabric store)
Flower to fit in pot

HERE'S WHAT YOU DO

Starting at the bottom side of the pot, apply a thick coating of glue about 2 inches at a time. Begin wrapping the floss adding glue and changing colors as desired. Use all 6 strands of floss. At the top lip work in the end of a purchased tassel. Cut the braid in two pieces and glue to the top rim over the embroidery floss. Put flower in pot.

Pastel Sugar Canes

QUICK AS A WINK

Here's a sweet idea that even gets sweeter. Start with pure white candy canes. Melt white chocolate in a double boiler and dip the curved end of the candy cane into the white chocolate. Sprinkle with colored sugar or colored sprinkles before the chocolate hardens. Lay on waxed paper to dry. Wrap in cellophane and tie with a ribbon for a quick and pretty candy gift.

Artful Magnets

Painted in the classic style of reverse painting, these tiny works of art are so easy to make you'll want the whole family to help. Use the tiny patterns we have given you or create your own. Remember to paint towards the center of the flat marble because these little pieces of artwork are magically magnified.

Here's What You Need
Clear half marbles (available at crafts, discount, or floral shops)
Small paintbrushes
Paints suitable for glass painting (available at art, crafts, and discount stores)
Disposable foam plate
3/4-inch circle magnets (available at crafts and discount stores)
Thick white crafts glue
Tiny plastic box (available at crafts stores)
Red cording

Here's What You Do
The clear half marbles usually come in a small bag. Choose the largest and clearest ones. Be sure they are clean and dry. Place a small amount of each color of paint on the disposable plate. Refer to the patterns, *left*, for ideas. Painting on the flat side of the marble, paint the front of the design first. For example, if you are painting the Christmas tree, paint the ornaments (dots) first. Let that dry. Then paint the green part of the tree over the dots. Let dry. Now, paint in a background color that accents the design. (We chose pink.) Let the background color dry. Glue a magnet to the back of the finished painted piece. Place several magnets in a tiny box and tie with a cording bow.

Gather up some of Grandma's vintage handkerchiefs and sewing trims to adorn these shapely felt stockings. The hankie is folded and tacked to the top of the simple stocking and the buttons and buckles are glued on for a stunning Christmas look.

Hankie Stockings

HERE'S WHAT YOU NEED

(For each stocking)

1/3 yard of colored felt

Tracing paper; pencil

Scissors

Sewing thread

Vintage handkerchief to accent or match felt color

Iron

1/2 yard of 1/4-inch-wide satin ribbon for the hanger

Old buttons and buckles

Hot-glue gun and hot glue sticks

HERE'S WHAT YOU DO

Enlarge the desired stocking pattern, *pages 115-117*, onto tracing paper or enlarge on a copy machine to 200%.

Cut out the pattern and transfer to the felt. Cut out two stocking pattern pieces from the felt. Using a matching sewing thread, sew the two felt stockings together with wrong sides facing stitching about 1/2-inch from the edge. You can use a sewing machine or you can stitch them by hand using a simple running stitch. Leave the top open.

To make the hankie cuff, choose a handkerchief that has a pretty corner and has colors that match the felt that you have chosen. Vintage hankies are easy to find at flea markets and antique stores and are inexpensive to buy. Iron the hankie flat. Fold the hankie diagonally and iron. To create the look of the cuff as we did on the pink and red stockings, turn the top fold down about two inches facing the point creating the appearance of a cuff. To create a look as we did on the blue stocking, turn the cuff under leaving the point of the stocking on the top. Iron the hankie again. Lay the folded hankie at the top of the felt stocking. Fold the ends to the back and tack with sewing thread using little stitches to hold.

Using little stitches, sew the two ends of the 1/4-inch ribbon together and place inside at the corner for a hanger. Choose buttons and buckles that accent the colors of the felt and the hankie that you used. Arrange them on the stocking. We chose a favorite button or buckle and accented the hankie. After you have decided on the arrangement, hot-glue in place.

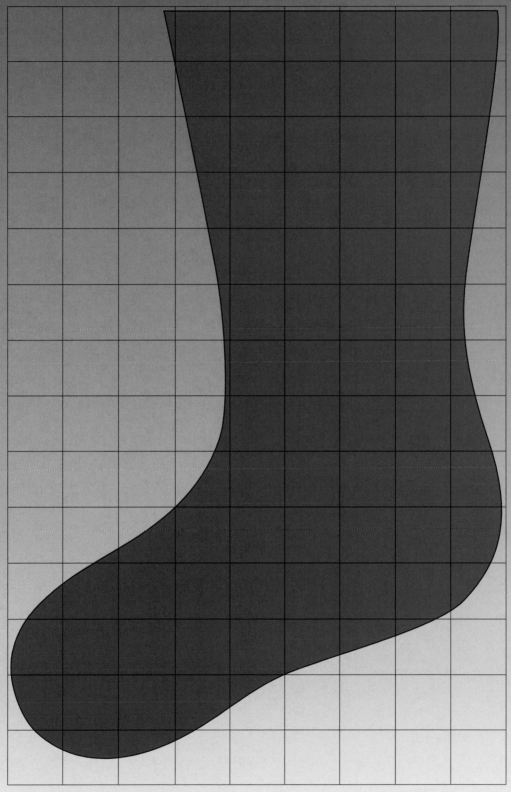

1 SQUARE = 1 INCH

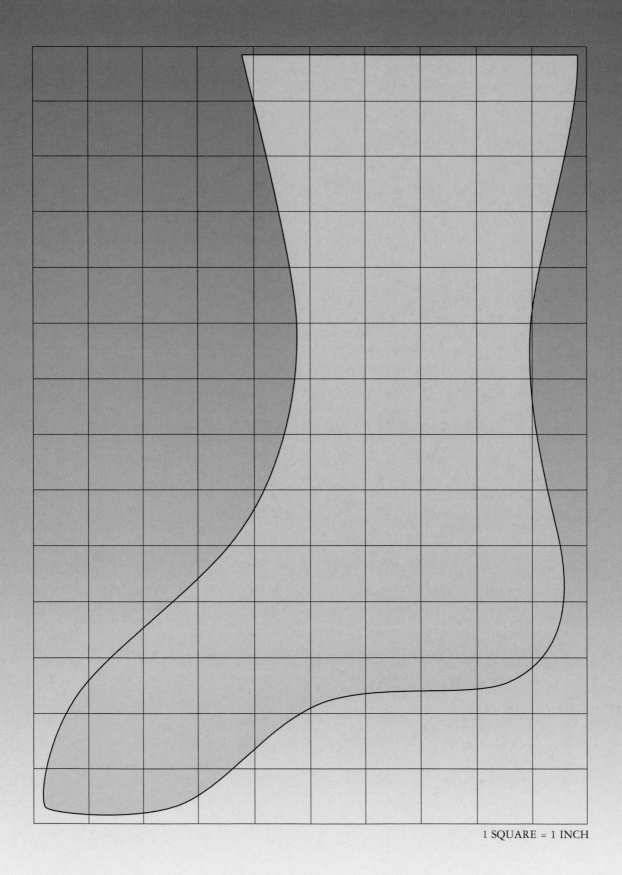

1 SQUARE = 1 INCH

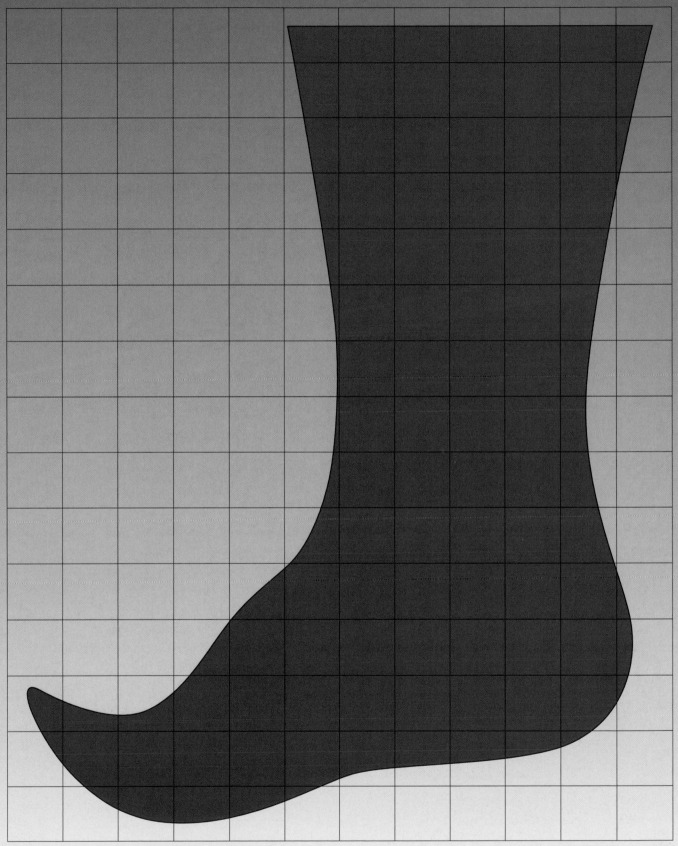

1 SQUARE = 1 INCH

117

Time for Friends Clock

QUICK AS A WINK

For that young person on your Christmas list, create a clock that will surely be placed in a spot of importance. Choose a clock that has a smooth surface and little decoration. Using a permanent metallic marker (available at crafts and discount stores), write the names of friends and favorite people all around the clock face. Let the marker dry.

QUICK AS A WINK

It may be winter, but the first signs of spring are always appreciated. Purchase narcissus bulbs and place with the root side down in a shallow dish that has been filled with tiny pebbles. Water the bulbs. (Narcissus bulbs need no dirt to grow.) Cover the pebbles with small ornaments and present as a lovely living gift.

Living Beauty

Playful Purse

What little girl wouldn't love this sweet little purse disguised as a fancy glove? It is so easy to make and is sure to be filled with all kinds of secret treasures.

HERE'S WHAT YOU NEED

A single one-size-fits-all brightly colored glove
Polyfiberfil stuffing
Sewing needle
Matching thread
2 pairs of large snaps
Hot-glue gun and hot-glue sticks
6 large jewels; play ring
Beading thread or dental floss
Colored beads

HERE'S WHAT YOU DO

Stuff each finger with polyester fiberfill until each one is plump and gently full.

Thread a sewing needle with matching colored thread and hand sew an even stitch line across the glove, closing in the stuffing at the base of each finger next to the palm.

Sew two pairs of large snaps securely onto the inside of the cuff of the glove. Hot-glue three large jewels to the outside of the cuff on each side. Slide the play ring on the glove finger and glue. Thread about 25 inches of beading thread or dental floss onto a needle. Begin on one side of cuff of glove. Securely knot the thread and sew several loops into the glove.

Begin stringing beads onto the thread in any random order of color. String enough beads to make a handle approximately 10 inches long. Carry the beaded strand to the end of the cuff, pulling it through until the beads lay firmly without puckering or leaving an open space of thread. Sew thread through several times, securing it firmly. To complete the other half of the handle, add more beads onto the string until it is the same length as the strand.

When it is the right length secure it at the same point where the beaded string began. Sew several loops of thread through until it is secure.

Fish Bowl Friends

Swimming happily in their own polka dot fish bowl, these fish will be happy to become part of the family on Christmas morning.

HERE'S WHAT YOU NEED
Fish bowl
Paints for painting on glass
Pencils with new eraser
Disposable foam plate
Narrow ribbon

HERE'S WHAT YOU DO
Wash and dry the fish bowl. Lay it down on the table and work on one side at a time.

Pour some of the paint onto the plate. Using the eraser end of the pencil, dip the pencil into the paint and make the polka dots where desired. Do all of one color at a time, leaving space between for the next color. Let the paint dry. Follow the manufacturer's directions for setting the paint. This oftentimes requires baking in the oven.

When the glass paint is cured, tie the ribbons around the top, add a tag if desired, and fill with water and goldfish.

Cookies for the Artist

For that budding artist on your list, here's an idea that will bring smiles. Oh-so-big sugar cookies are covered with primary hues and colorful sugar. The bright paint can has its own clever personality.

HERE'S WHAT YOU NEED
New empty quart-size paint can (available at paint stores for about $1.00)
Acrylic paints in bright colors
Disposable plate; paintbrushes; towel
Plastic coated wire in bright colors
18-inch square piece of red cellophane (available at crafts and discount stores)
Cookies decorated with brightly colored frosting and sugar (We used Grandma's Sugar Cookie recipe on page 86)

HERE'S WHAT YOU DO
Wash and dry the new paint can. Prop in at an angle on an old towel. Put desired colors of paint on the disposable plate. Load the paintbrush with one color paint. Paint a little around the top of the can and let it run down the side. Repeat using other colors of paint. Do one side of the can at a time letting the paints mix together as they drip. Let the paint dry.

Take the handle out of the can. Thread the colored wire through the handle holes twisting around a pencil to make it curl. Bring the wire around the top forming a handle. Or, you can leave the handle in the can and twist the wire around it.

Push the piece of cellophane down into the can and fill with cookies. We made our cookies round and thick and frosted them with bright frosting and sugar.

Sweet Baby Toys

You'll be the favorite, when you give baby a little stuffed pet to squeeze and love. Made just to fit baby's little hands, the features are embroidered on the fabric giving each one a personality all its own.

HERE'S WHAT YOU NEED
Tracing paper; pencil
Transfer paper in blue and red
*¹/4 yard **each** of yellow, pink, blue, and green pastel bathrobe velour*
Straight pins
Permanent markers in blue and red
DMC cotton embroidery floss: 601, 604, 726, 782, 797, 3839, 3847, 3851
Embroidery needle; scissors; tweezers
Sewing thread to match fabrics; needle
Polyester batting
*¹/2 yard **each** of ¹/4-inch-wide pink, green, yellow, and blue pastel ribbon*

NOTE: Add ¹/4-inch cutting line to each character.

HERE'S WHAT YOU DO
Trace pattern of character, *pages 126-127*, onto tracing paper. Add another line ¹/4 inch all the way around to indicate the cutting line.

On a single layer of fabric (wrong side up) pin the transfer carbon and tracing of character. Trace around cutting and sewing edges. Remove papers. Fold fabric double with right sides facing. Pin together. Cut out. Remove pins.

With right side facing up on one fabric, place tracing of character to line up exactly with cut edge. Slip transfer paper between fabric and tracing. Trace all embroidery lines. Remove papers. Go over any lines with permanent marker to clarify. Embroider all features (all stitches are worked in 3 strands of floss). Place both sides of fabric together, pin in place (with wrong sides facing). Stitch on stitching line leaving bottom of character open. Trim fabric, clip at corners, turn inside out. Use tweezers to insert stuffing in ears, arms, and legs. Blindstitch bottom closed. Sew a length of ribbon on neck and form a bow with a separate piece of ribbon. Hand stitch in place. Be sure to stitch down entire ribbon and bow for safety.

125

SATIN STITCH

FRENCH KNOT

A B

CROSS STITCH

D
BF
E
G C
A
H

RUNNING STITCH

E D C B A

BACKSTITCH

G
EH
CF
D
A
B

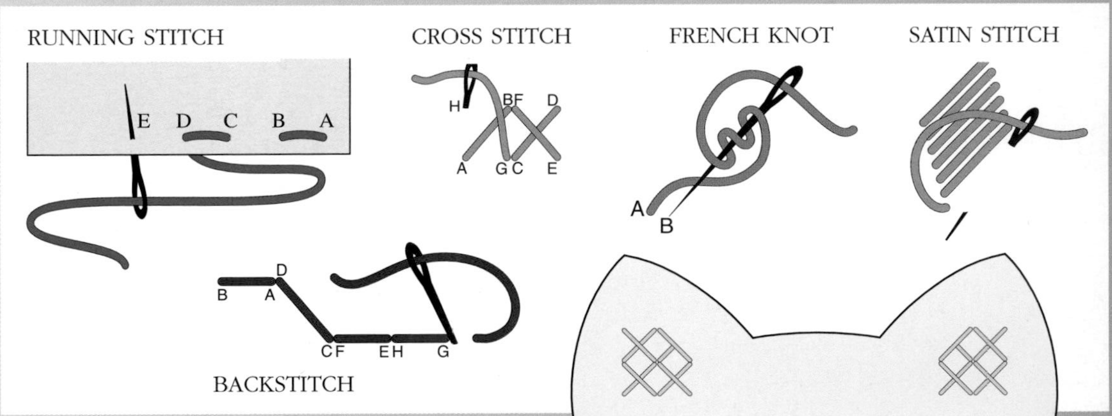

BUNNY C
Cross-stitch
✕ 3839 Light royal blue (3X)
Backstitch
╱ 797 Royal blue (3X)
Straight stitch
╱ 797 Royal blue (3X)
╱ 3839 Light royal blue (3X)
Running stitch
╱ 797 Royal blue (3X)

CAT B
Cross-stitch
✕ 726 Light topaz (3X)
Backstitch
╱ 782 Medium topaz (3X)
Straight stitch
╱ 726 Light topaz (3X)
╱ 782 Medium topaz (3X)
French knot
● 782 Medium topaz (3X)
Running stitch
╱ 782 Medium topaz (3X)

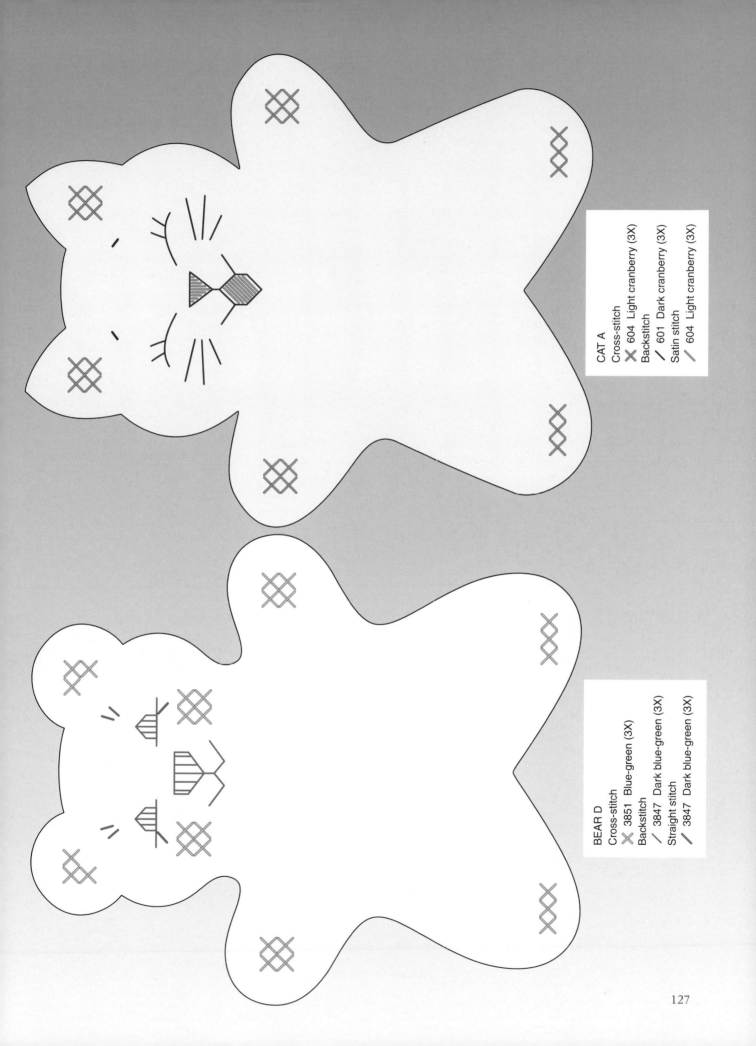

CAT A
Cross-stitch
X 604 Light cranberry (3X)
Backstitch
╱ 601 Dark cranberry (3X)
Satin stitch
╱ 604 Light cranberry (3X)

BEAR D
Cross-stitch
X 3851 Blue-green (3X)
Backstitch
╱ 3847 Dark blue-green (3X)
Straight stitch
╱ 3847 Dark blue-green (3X)

Spicy Soap Holder

Made from sticks of cinnamon and red leather lacing, this clever soap holder adds spice to any clean-up area. Add a star gift tag and greeting and your gift is compete.

HERE'S WHAT YOU NEED
Eight 4-inch-long cinnamon sticks
Small sheet of plastic foam such as
Styrofoam (to hold sticks for wrapping)

2 yards of red leather lacing
One small piece of red leather; scissors
Black permanent marker

HERE'S WHAT YOU DO
Push the cinnamon sticks into the plastic foam 1/2-inch apart so they stand up vertically. Cut the leather lacing in half. Leaving about a 2-inch tail, begin at one end about 1/2 inch down from the top and wrap one of the leather lacing strips completely around all of

the sticks. Wrap the long piece around the tail and begin wrapping under and over the leather lacing that lays across the sticks, wrapping two times between each stick. See diagram, *below*. Turn the sticks over, push into the Styrofoam and repeat as for other side. Tuck ends in. Cut off excess lacing. Cut a star from the leather piece. Write greeting with marker. Tie on holder.

QUICK AS A WINK

A purchased amaryllis becomes a gift of real beauty by adding a few simple touches. After the bloom has begun to sprout, encircle it with colored marbles and tie a bow of beautiful ribbon around the flower container.

Marbled Amaryllis

Making the Perfect Bow

Part of the secret of a perfect bow is to use plenty of ribbon and to choose ribbon that is suitable for the look you want to create. Follow these easy instructions and you'll be surprised how easy bow-making can be.

HERE'S WHAT YOU DO

Decide what kind of bow you want for your package. Do you want it to be soft and elegant or to stand up and be fresh and crisp. The type of ribbon that you choose will give you the results you want.

Wire-edge or wired ribbon is the best to use for a traditional bow. A stiffer ribbon will create a crisp bow and sheer ribbon gives a softer look. Grosgrain or soft satin ribbon does not work well for traditional bow making.

You will also need about 12 inches of a thin wire (24-gauge works well), for each bow for twisting around the middle and securing the center loop. If you are

using 1- or 1½-wide ribbon, you will need about 3 yards of ribbon for a full bow. The photographs, *below and right*, show a 1½-inch wire-edge ribbon with a 5-inch bow. Wider ribbon takes more yardage and narrower ribbon takes less yardage.

1 *Leaving an 8-inch beginning tail, loop the ribbon back and forth accordion style. Make at least 5 loops. Leave about an 18-inch end tail.*

2 *Pinch the centers of the loops together.*

3 *Twist the thin wire around the center of the loops. Do not trim the wire.*

4 *Using the end tail make a small loop near the center. Pull one of the wire ends down and around the loop to the back and twist with other wire end, securing the bow loop center.*

5 *Pull the bow loops apart and trim the tails.*

Wrapping the Perfect Package

A beautifully wrapped package is the final touch to that well-thought-out gift. Sometimes that perfect gift cooperates and fits nicely in a square box. But sometimes that special gift needs some creative help to be wrapped beatifully. Here are some ideas for wrapping all kind of gifts plus some tips for making each wrap package-perfect.

HERE'S WHAT YOU DO

There are so many wonderful papers, boxes, bags, cellophanes, tissues, and ribbons available today on the market. This makes wrapping gifts easier and more fun than ever.

First, analyze the shape of your gift and decide if it will fit nicely into a square or rectangular box. These are the easiest kinds of packages to wrap.

You can purchase cardboard boxes for wrapping at discount stores, party stores, and even department stores. Choose a box that is sturdy and leaves enough room to add tissue or shred around the gift.

Choose a high-quality wrapping paper that will allow for crisp folds. Avoid metallic papers that crack when folded or thin papers that tear easily.

Cut a piece of wrapping paper big enough to fit around the box and overlap about three inches. Refer to the photographs, *below,* for tips on wrapping a square or rectangular box.

1 *Set the box in the middle of the paper. Tape one end of the paper to the box. Fold back the other end of the paper about ¹/₂ inch and crease. Pull up and secure over the taped end.*

2 *Fold the sides of the paper in and down. Fold back the ends about ¹/₄ inch. Roll a piece of tape with the sticky side out and pull the ends up.*

3 *Crease all the edges of the paper where it meets the box by sliding your finger and pinching the paper along the edges of the box. This gives the package a clean, crisp look.*

1 *Cut a paper towel roll to the length desired. Put gifts or money in the roll. Lay the roll on a large square of patterned tissue paper. Tape down one side and roll the tissue around it. Secure with transparent tape.*

2 *Trim the ends with pinking shears. Tie ribbon at both ends pulling the tissue up tightly with the ribbon. Tie another knot. Trim the ribbon ends and curl the ribbon.*

Some gifts require a bit more planning to make them able to be wrapped. For small items such as jewelry, small odd-shaped toys, or money, try using a paper towel roll or other round tube. See the photographs, *above,* for wrapping small items in a tube.

For large odd-shaped packages, try using cellophane, fabric or combining the two together. Cellophane can be purchased at party stores or floral shops. During the holidays it is also available at grocery stores or any place where fruit baskets are made.

Cellophane is inexpensive, but it requires a large piece to pull up and around odd-shaped gifts. Large pieces of colorful fabric can be pulled up and around the gift as well. See the photograph, *right,* for tips on wrapping odd-shaped gifts.

1 *Cut out a very large square of fabric or cellophane using pinking shears or regular scissors. (We layered them together and treated them as one piece). Pull up all four corners at a time and secure with a rubber band. Tie a bow around the rubber band and trim the ribbon ends. Trim off the top if desired.*

More Ways to Give

Sometimes the extra thoughtfulness in creating the perfect gift is all it takes to make it the one that is remembered for years to come. Here are a few ideas that will make your gift-giving easier and more memorable.

🍃 Make every wrapped package special by attaching a special trinket to the bow to personalize the gift. Try using wrapped candies, ornaments, toys, jewelry, or other unique items to add an unexpected twist.

🍃 When doing holiday shopping, remember to pick up everything you need for gift wrapping. Gift bags, wrapping paper, bows, ribbon, tape, bubble wrap, gift tags, cellophane, tissue paper, and boxes are a few of the necessities.

🍃 When mailing holiday gifts, be sure to use appropriate packing and boxes. If you do not have them on hand, take your gifts to a mailing store and they will do it for you. Many catalogue companies will mail your gifts directly for you at no extra cost.

🍃 Avoid long lines at the post office by mailing out-of-town gifts early. Be sure and put the address inside as well as outside the box.

🍃 Keep Christmas cards from year to year to recycle and snip portions for gift tags. They can also be decoupaged onto gift boxes for colorful holiday containers.

🍃 Remember thoughtful neighbors at Christmas time with a small, meaningful gift. Some ideas are a homemade certificate for free snow shoveling, fresh baked bread, or a pretty holiday plant.

🍃 If you run short of holiday wrap, use fabric or a paper doily or place mat. Stickers can be used in place of tape. And a sprig of greenery makes a lovely bow.

🍃 Keep a list handy and record all of the gifts you receive through the mail. Be sure to send written thank yous when the holidays are over.

🍃 Express your appreciation to people who make your life easier throughout the year. Give small gifts to your mail deliverer, hair stylist, co-workers, and other special people you want to thank.

🍃 When carrying a load of gifts, use a basket with a handle for small gifts and a laundry basket to carry the larger ones.

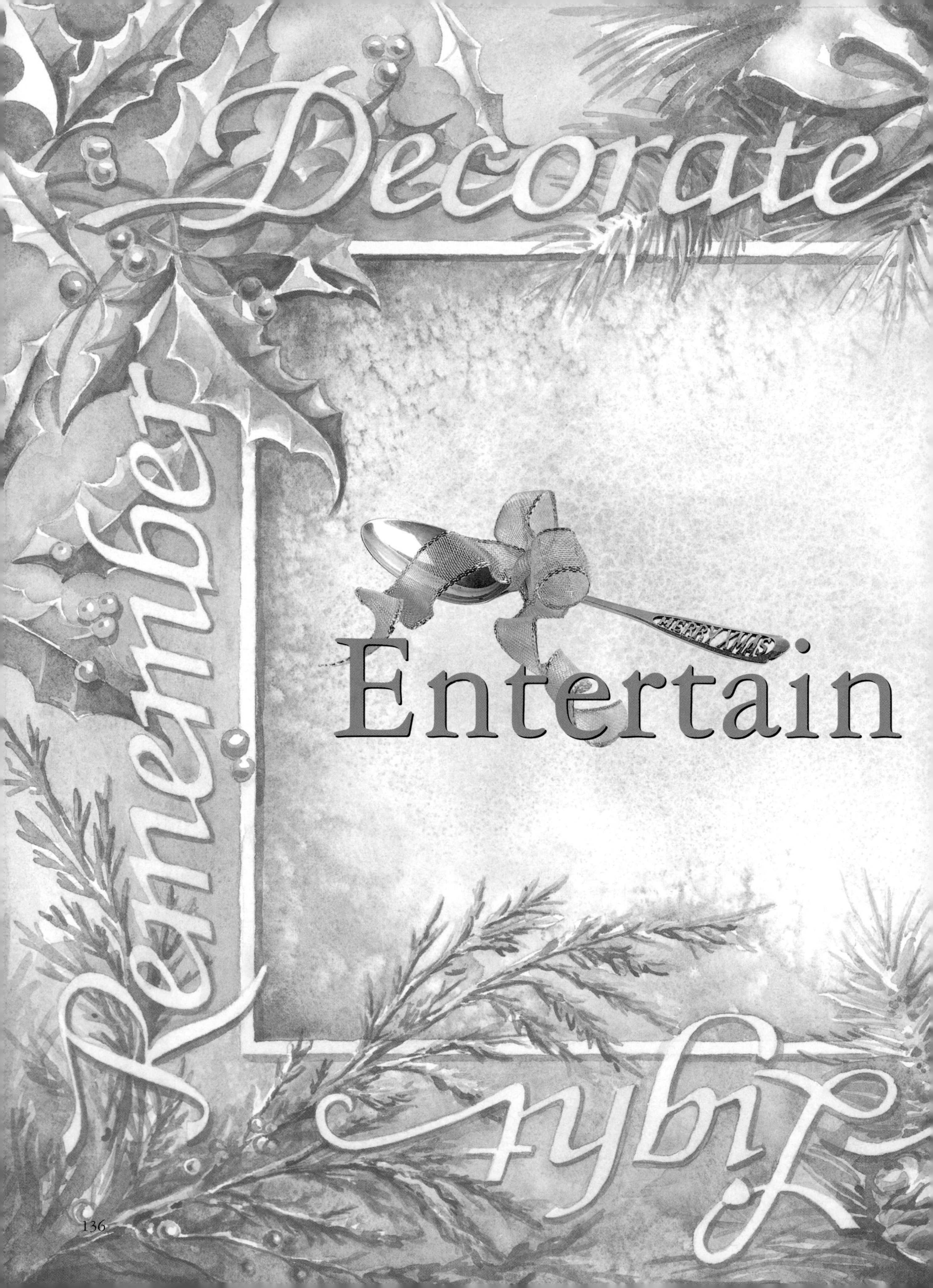
Decorate
Remember
Light
MERRY XMAS

Entertain

Greet Nourish Give Entertain

Having friends and loved ones come to your home for the holidays is one of the most rewarding times of all. With easy-to-make ideas you can welcome your guests at the door with a relaxed smile and a warm heart—ready to share the holiday fun together.

Christmas Topiary

Create this holiday topiary in unexpected colors—or colors to match your Christmas buffet table. Spray-painted ornaments are combined with tiny Christmas balls to create the multicolored topiary. Add accordion-folded sheer ribbon to finish the soft holiday look.

HERE'S WHAT YOU NEED

Small, round Christmas ornaments in two sizes

1 yard of fine wire

Spray paint in desired colors (suitable for use on glass)

4-inch plastic foam ball, such as Styrofoam

11-inch length of 1/4-inch-diameter dowel; white spray paint

Hot-glue gun and hot-glue sticks

Small piece of Styrofoam to fit into flowerpot

5-inch-wide terra-cotta flowerpot

1 1/2-inch-wide sheer ribbon

HERE'S WHAT YOU DO

Thread the larger ornaments to be sprayed on the wire so they are suspended for spray painting. Lightly spray paint the ornaments. It is fine if some of the color of the original ornaments shows through. This will make the ornaments have more dimension. Spray paint the Styrofoam ball and the dowel the same color as the ornaments. Spray the flowerpot white. Let all the pieces dry thoroughly.

Put the dowel in the bottom of the Styrofoam ball. Carefully begin hot gluing the ornaments to the Styrofoam as tightly together as possible. Work on one side of the ball at a time. When all the balls have been glued on, add shiny smaller ornaments between the other balls where desired.

Glue the small piece of Styrofoam inside the flowerpot. Push the bottom of the dowel into the Styrofoam. Glue to secure.

Place tiny ornaments loosely on the top of the pot. Accordion-pleat the ribbon and arrange in the flowerpot over the balls.

QUICK AS A WINK

Holiday pins are still worn today, but a Christmas pin was a must on every wool coat years ago. Enjoy those dear jewelry trims at each place setting by displaying them in candles, or pinning them on napkins and place cards. We warmed the stick portion of the pin with a flame and gently pushed it into the candle.

Ornament Place Cards

Everyone will know their place when they find their name displayed on their own take-home ornament, each standing tall in its own beaded holder. So easy to do, you can make a whole set in an evening.

HERE'S WHAT YOU NEED
2 purchased ornaments in desired color
   (we chose purple)
Rubber cement; gold spray paint
Gold permanent fine-line marker
2 extra hangers from old ornaments
Two 2-inch square beveled mirrors
Six inches of ¹/₈-inch tiny gold bead
   garland
Thick white crafts glue; scissors
Purchased place cards

HERE'S WHAT YOU DO
We made the ornament place cards in sets. One is a reverse color of the other. *For the purple with gold star ornament,* draw criss-cross stars on it using the gold marker. *For the purple-starred ornament,* use rubber cement to draw criss-cross stars on the ornament. Let the rubber cement dry. After it is dry, spray paint the ball gold. Let dry. Using your finger, very carefully rub the rubber cement from the ball. The purple from the ornament will show through.

For the place card holder take the hanger top out of the decorated ornament. Take out the wire loop.

Now, take just the wire loop hanger top from an old ornament. Squeeze the bottom two wires together on both loops and put them through the same holes into the top of the original one. Put the top back on the decorated ornament. The two loops create a holder for the name card.

To make the ornament stand, cut 3 inches of the beaded garland. Form a circle with the beads and glue to the center of the mirror. Let the glue dry. Place the ornament on the circle of beads.

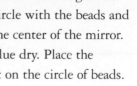

Clever Christmas Candleholders

Create a conversation piece as well as a centerpiece by making these oh-so-showy artichoke candleholders. With just a little paint and candles to match, these clever and colorful pieces can be made in no time.

HERE'S WHAT YOU NEED

Two artichokes
Taper candles
Small sharp knife
Candleholders
Wooden or metal skewer
Metallic gold spray paint
Red transparent metallic spray paint
 or other desired color (available at
 crafts and hobby shops)
White crafts glue
Yellow large and small rhinestones

HERE'S WHAT YOU DO

Purchase nice, unbruised, fresh artichokes with symmetrical shapes. Choose tapered candles that compliment the color you choose to paint the artichokes. Use a small sharp knife and cut out the center leaves to hold the candle firmly. Leave the base stem long enough to insert into a candleholder.

Insert a skewer into the stem end of the artichoke so you can easily hold it while painting. Spray-paint the artichoke metallic gold first. Let it dry.

Spray over the gold the color of your choice. We used a transparent red metallic spray paint. Using a transparent paint over the gold paint gives a metallic look. Allow the paints to dry thoroughly. Glue the small yellow rhinestones to the tips of artichoke leaves with white crafts glue. You may use larger rhinestones on the tips of the lower leaves and use smaller rhinestones towards the top ones.

Insert the candles firmly into the center of the artichoke. Place the base of the artichokes into the candleholders. Be creative when selecting the candleholders. You can pick several shapes and heights to make your centerpiece more interesting.

The painted artichokes will keep for about two weeks depending on the particular artichoke and climate conditions. Of course, after painting, the artichokes would not be edible.

Snowman Candy Cups

These clever no-melt snowmen will make everyone smile as they wish your guests a Happy Holiday. Fill these little fellows with brightly wrapped candies and place one by each table setting for some Christmas fun.

HERE'S WHAT YOU NEED

Large bell cups (found in the dry floral section of crafts stores)
Drill and 1/8-inch drill bit
Crayola® Model Magic® clay
Acrylic paints in iridescent pale blue, orange, pink, and black
Paintbrush; pencil
Thick white crafts glue
Iridescent white chenille stems
Purchased black felt hat to fit size of bell cup

HERE'S WHAT YOU DO

Carefully twist wire stem on the bell cup and remove. Drill a hole 1/2-inch from the rim of the bell cup. Drill a second hole opposite the first.

Using a marble-size piece of clay, form a carrot-shape nose. Let the clay air dry.

Paint the bell cup iridescent pale blue. Paint the clay nose orange. Let dry. Paint the snowman's cheeks pink. Let dry. Using the patterns, *below*, for inspiration, draw a face using pencil. Paint over the pencil marks using black paint. Let it dry.

Glue the nose in place. Let the glue dry. Poke the chenille stem through the holes in the bell cup. Carefully shape into a handle. Place the felt hat on top of the snowman. Fill the cups with wrapped Christmas candies.

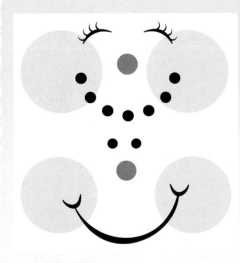

Take-Home Tumblers

QUICK AS A WINK

Choose glasses that complement your table setting and then make them even more special by writing the names of your guests using a gold paint permanent marker. Many are available at crafts and home centers. Be sure that the markers are permanent when used on glassware so the glasses can be washed.

Centerpiece in Red and Green

Mix sets of colorful dinnerware to create your own personal centerpiece built to the height and dimension of your holiday table. We used crystal plates in various sizes and patterns and combined them with depression-age goblets, sherbets, and a sugar bowl to make our outstanding centerpiece.

HERE'S WHAT YOU NEED

5 goblets of the same height

4 sherbets of the same height

1 large clear round plate about 15 inches in diameter

1 medium clear round plate about 12 inches in diameter

1 small clear round plate about 8 inches in diameter

1 sugar bowl without lid

Cut roses, rose heads, and baby's breath

HERE'S WHAT YOU DO

Choose dishes that complement your dinner dishes and tablecloth.

Work directly on the table. Do not try to move the centerpiece after it is set up.

Start by inverting the goblets on the large plate with four around the edges and one in the middle. Now place the middle-size plate on the goblets. The goblets act as a pedestal. Repeat by placing the next four sherbets on top of the middle-size plate. Top with the small plate and the sugar bowl.

Add water to the plates. The plates will not hold a lot of water but enough to float the rose heads and baby's breath.

Fill the sugar bowl with water and arrange the roses.

Napkin Tie-Ups

QUICK AS A WINK

Make your napkin holders a special part of the table setting by creating your own clever tie ons. Let the guests take these beautiful additions home with them as part of the holiday fun. A wishbone dusted with glitter is a good luck charm for the upcoming year. Grandma's vintage jewelry wraps the napkin beautifully as does the tiny antique cup with a golden ribbon curled through the handle.

Flowers Under Glass

QUICK AS A WINK

To show off those lovely pieces of clear glass that so often get overlooked, try stacking one dish inside another. Here we put a crystal goblet inside a brandy snifter and surrounded the goblet with small ornaments. Fill the goblet with water and add fresh flowers for a most unexpected and delightful centerpiece.

Lights All Around

Your guests will feel more connected when they find their names beautifully written on snow white Christmas tree lights all tied together with a single satin ribbon. Add a simple painted motif to each name card for an added touch of style.

HERE'S WHAT YOU NEED
White replacement Christmas tree lights
Pencil
Paints suitable for glass painting
Disposable foam plate
Fine-tipped paintbrush
¹/4-inch-wide ribbon in two colors

HERE'S WHAT YOU DO
Wash and dry the light bulbs. Try not to touch the glass before painting. Very lightly write the name of each guest on the light bulbs with a pencil. Have some light bulbs facing one way and some the opposite way.

Put the desired colors of paints on the disposable plate. Go over the pencil marks with paint using a fine-tipped paintbrush. Add designs to the bulbs such as evergreen, holly, or ribbons. Allow the paint to dry thoroughly.

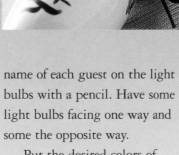

Tie small bows at the top of the bulb if desired. Then, tie all of the bulbs together using a long piece of ¹/4-inch-wide ribbon leaving enough room between the bulbs so each bulb can lay in front of the guest's place setting.

When the guests leave for home, cut the bulbs apart and give the bulb as a memento of the dinner party.

Burst-of-Color Centerpiece

Simple, yet beautifully unusual, this painted pineapple is a stunning display of color and pattern. Displayed with a few tiny ornaments mixed with greens and beads, the centerpiece is sure to be the talk of the holiday table.

HERE'S WHAT YOU NEED
Pineapple
Newspapers
Gold spray paint
Acrylic metallic paints in green,
*   magenta, orange, and purple*
Disposable foam plate
3/8-inch flat paintbrush
Water

HERE'S WHAT YOU DO
Choose a pineapple with a uniform shape and good leaves that aren't bent or broken. Make sure it is clean and dry.

Lay down newspapers for spray painting. Spray-paint leaves first with gold. Spray several light coats until it is thoroughly covered. Let the pineapple dry. Some of the paint will probably spray onto the body of the pineapple. That paint will be covered by the colored paint. Place small amounts of all the colors of acrylic paint, (about the size of a quarter) onto a plate. We used metallic green, magenta, orange, and purple. Use a 3/8-inch flat brush to paint sections. Paint a random pattern or paint in rows of color. Let the paint dry and paint a second coat if needed.

Arrange the pineapple with other small decorations, such as ornaments or bells. Add fresh greens and display in a special dish or on a cake plate. The pineapple will keep for about a week or two depending on the ripeness of the fruit. The paint will act as a sealer and will keep the pineapple longer than if it wasn't painted. Of course, the pineapple will not be edible after painting.

More Ways to Entertain

*G*etting ready for special holiday entertaining should be as much fun for you as for your guests. Here are some easy ideas that are sure to please everyone.

❧ Spruce up a holiday table by placing a candy cane or truffle on each guest's plate.

❧ When serving punch, place a wreath on the table first. Place the punch bowl in the center of the wreath and arrange holly, small ornaments, and other holiday items in the fresh greens.

❧ Mismatched crystal can combine to make a glorious impression. Collect pieces you like from flea markets, garage sales, antique shops, and second-hand or thrift shops. Set the table using the one-of-a-kind pieces.

❧ When guests will be staying overnight, surprise them with a basket of goodies left on their beds or in the bathroom. Select items such as shampoo, soap, cotton balls, hand lotion, and toothpaste.

🍃 Lighting can set the mood for your gathering. Dim the lights or replace bright bulbs with dimmer versions to create soft lighting.

🍃 Be creative with your furniture groupings when planning a holiday party. Rearrange your chairs and couches in groups to encourage merry conversations.

🍃 Since visitors often migrate to the kitchen, be sure to dress it up for the holidays. Add festive lighting or a small holiday collection to bring cheer to the room.

🍃 Personalize a glass for each guest before they arrive. During the gathering each person will know where their very own take-home glass is and when it needs a refill.

🍃 For large parties, fill big copper, tin, or decorative plastic tubs with crushed ice (or snow) and place bottled or canned drinks inside to keep them cold.

🍃 Look in the newspaper or ask the local music teacher for names of people who could play live music at your gathering. Oftentimes a harpist, pianist, or violinist will come and play for an hourly rate.

🍃 Hire a neighborhood teenager to come to the party to help care for the younger guests. Be sure there are toys and food appropriate for all ages.

Decorate

Remember

Light

Light

Greet

The magic of the holidays comes alive with the twinkling of Christmas lights that signal that the holidays have arrived. Whether it be the elegance of a candle lit room, luminarias that light the walkway, or the soft light needed to read those glorious Christmas stories, you'll find beautiful ideas to light your way.

Natural Lighting

QUICK AS A WINK

Here are some quick and lovely candle ideas that use the
natural colors in fruits and flowers to accentuate the candles.
Stack square glass dishes and fill them with cranberries for a
rich holiday accent, or slice lemons and limes to encircle a
floating candle. We added a pinch of glitter. Simple pink rose
petals are strewn about our peachy pink candle trio.

Starry Night Luminarias

Castaway jars and golden spray paint combine to create these twinkling luminarias. Make them by the dozens for the walkway or in sets of two or three to make any room of the house shine.

HERE'S WHAT YOU NEED

Old glass jars such as peanut butter
*   or pickle jars*
2 pennies
Old paintbrush
Rubber cement
Gold spray paint
Gold cording
Gold glitter
Gold beads by the yard
Thick white crafts glue

HERE'S WHAT YOU DO

Wash and dry the jar. Lay the jar down on one side and keep it from rolling by placing a penny on both sides of the jar. Paint stars on the jar using the rubber cement. Simply dip the brush into the rubber cement and paint on the glue as if it was paint. The stars can be made using lines or you can make them solid. They need not be perfect or even the same. Let the glue dry thoroughly. This will take about 15 minutes.

Spray-paint the jar gold. Paint directly over the stars. Let the paint dry thoroughly. (This could take a few hours or overnight.) Using your finger, carefully rub off the rubber cement. Trim the jar tops by gluing on cording, glitter, or beads. Add a candle in each jar.

Lighting
Companions

QUICK AS A WINK

Pick your favorite candle shape and color and look for unexpected items to accent each one. Pearls add an elegant twist to a plain white candle and red jewels on yellow and blue plates make the primary color scheme shine. Dozens of jingle bells or colorful vintage Christmas lights make an ordinary candle spectacular.

Constant Light

Oil lamps were a steady burning and constant light so reliable and depended upon a century ago. Make these lovely lamps to add a touch of shimmering beauty to any room this holiday season.

HERE'S WHAT YOU NEED

Bottle with flat sides and narrow neck

White flat marbles (available in the floral department of crafts and discount stores)

Strong glue adhesive such as Liquid Nails

Narrow white cording

Small pearls (available at crafts stores)

Toothpick

Wick, ring, and tube for making oil lamps (available at crafts stores)

Funnel; oil made for oil lamps (available at discount stores)

HERE'S WHAT YOU DO

Choose an interestingly shaped bottle that has flat sides. It must have a narrow neck to accommodate the oil lamp tube and metal ring.

Old perfume bottles work well and can be found easily at flea markets.

Be sure the bottle is clean and dry. Using a toothpick, dab the adhesive onto the back of the flat marble and affix it to the side of the bottle. Continue until the entire bottle is covered. Work on one side at a time waiting until the marbles are set before moving to the other side.

Glue the cording around the neck and the pearls on the bottle ledge. Slip the wick into the glass tube holder. The wick should be long enough to touch the bottom of the bottle. Set the ring on top of the bottle and place the tube into the ring. Pull the wick up barely above the glass tube.

Remove the top carefully and using a funnel fill the bottle with oil made for oil lamps. Replace the top. Never leave a burning candle unattended.

Frosty Candle Ring

A circle of glittered
snowflakes are accented
with silver ornaments to
make a wreath that's as
pretty as new fallen snow.

HERE'S WHAT YOU NEED
*Purchased glitter-coated snowflakes
in various sizes and shapes*

Scissors
Hot-glue gun
Hot-glue sticks
Small silver glass ornaments
1-inch-wide silver ribbon

HERE'S WHAT YOU DO
Arrange the snowflakes in a circle,
reserving the smaller ones to place
on top. Cut ¼- to ½-inch-long

pieces of glue sticks to place under
the small snowflakes to add
dimension. Remove the glue stick
pieces and small snowflakes.

Use hot glue to attach the
snowflakes in a circle, making sure
edges overlap for stability. Glue the
short pieces of glue stick to
snowflake circle where smaller
snowflakes will be added. Glue small
snowflakes atop glue stick pieces.

Arrange silver ornaments
around the wreath and glue in
place. Tie a ribbon bow and glue
in place.

165

Merry Christmas Lampshade

The beautiful age old art of paper punching is the technique used to create light and shadow on this festive shade. We used a star pattern and a simple "Merry Christmas" to accent our shade, but any greeting or shape will work well to bring sparkling light to your holiday room.

HERE'S WHAT YOU NEED
Tracing paper
Pencil
Purchased lampshade
  (we chose an ecru shade that is
  3 1/4 inches across at the top and
  11 inches across at the bottom)
Transparent tape
T-pin

HERE'S WHAT YOU DO
Trace the patterns, below onto tracing paper. Cut around the patterns leaving about $1/2$ inch around each pattern. Arrange the patterns on the lampshade where desired. You can use the patterns more than once, or you can make multiples of each pattern. Tape the patterns in place. Using the T-pin, start poking holes through the shade. The holes should be about $1/8$ to $1/4$ inch apart. Continue poking holes until the pattern is completed. Remove the tissue paper.

Candles of Gold and Silver

With one simple technique, you can add sparkle to this elegant candle as well as its holder. Tiny wood pieces glued to glass add style to this beautiful piece.

HERE'S WHAT YOU NEED

Two 3/16-inch-thick 3 1/2×5-inch pieces of glass with sanded edges
Two 3/16-inch-thick 6×6-inch pieces of glass with sanded edges (available where glass is cut, such as hardware stores or glass stores)
Gold and silver leaf and leafing adhesive (available at crafts stores)
Paintbrush for applying adhesive
Thick brush for brushing off leaf
Thick white crafts glue
Four 1 1/4-inch wooden balls with flat edges
Four 1-inch wooden square pieces
Large candle

HERE'S WHAT YOU DO

One piece of each size glass, the wood base pieces, and the candle are all metallic leafed. The same process is used on all pieces. The gold or silver leaf comes in sheets and is very thin. You will be putting little pieces on at a time. You can use a lot of leaf (as on the glass) or very little (as on the candle). Wherever you apply adhesive is exactly where you will have the gold or silver leaf.

For all pieces, apply the leaf adhesive where you want the gold or silver to be. Allow the adhesive to dry to a tacky, but not wet, stage. You should not be able to wipe or smear it off with your finger.

When the adhesive is ready, begin to apply the gold and silver leaf using a small amount at a time. For a two-toned look (as on the glass) lay one color down first, leaving open uncovered areas. After the first color is down, complete covering the glass with the other color. Rub down all the leaf firmly but gently with your finger. Brush off extra leaf with large brush.

Apply the leaf adhesive to the candle or other surface using a paintbrush. Let the adhesive dry until tacky.

Apply the metallic leaf to the adhesive, working with small pieces at a time.

With crafts glue, affix leg pieces to the underside of each corner of the leafed glass pieces. The leafed side of glass should face upward, with legs underneath. Set the other matching clear glass on top of the leafed glass. Stack the glass pieces atop one another and place candle on top.

More Ways to
Light

Simple twinkling lights or softly lit candles are all it takes to show that Christmas is near. Here are some last-minute ideas to light up your home.

🍃 Wrap outdoor Christmas lights around a sled or wagon and set it outside to create a magical silhouette for the holidays.

🍃 Standard-size light bulbs come in a variety of colors and are available in home centers and discount stores. Try replacing outdoor bulbs with red or green for the holidays.

🍃 If you like to burn candles during the holidays, remember to clip the wicks before lighting and never leave a burning candle unattended.

🍃 Group white candles in a variety of clear glass and brass candleholders for an elegant centerpiece.

🍃 For an old-fashioned themed tree, use reproduction bubble lights, available in home centers. Tinsel draped over the branches adds the perfect antique-looking touch.

❦ To easily transform an ordinary pillar candle into a striking holiday decoration, gently push star-shaped studs into the surface of the candle.

❦ In warm-weather areas, place floating candles in fish bowls arranged alongside the walkway to make luminarias. If there is snow, place the snow inside the bowls nestled around the candles.

❦ For a glistening centerpiece, float a poinsettia head in a large rose bowl. Place floating candles around it and light them.

❦ To add holiday scents to your home, select candles that send wafts of pine, cranberry, or spice through the air.

❦ Look for simple and inexpensive lamp bases at home and discount stores. Dress them up for the holidays with red and green polka-dots of paint or an elegant gold tassel tied at the neck.

❦ Add battery-powered Christmas lights to baskets of pine cones or wreaths to add a touch of sparkle.

❦ Buy dozens of colored replacement Christmas bulbs and group them by color in clear bowls or fish bowls. Tuck greens around them and arrange them on the mantel or buffet.

Decorate

Remember

Remember

There is nothing quite so dear as the memories that Christmas brings. Choose to celebrate those Christmases past by displaying your collections in unique ways. It only takes a minute to arrange those special treasures of yesterday for your family to enjoy today.

Holiday Message

A vintage typewriter finds a clever place in your decorating scheme with a fresh coat of paint and a handwritten message from Santa himself. Simply spray paint the typewriter red and then hand paint the keys and trim a bright holiday gold.

HERE'S WHAT YOU NEED

Old typewriter
Red spray paint
Gold paint suitable for metal
Small paintbrushes
6×8-inch piece of gold or patterned paper
Black fine-line marker

HERE'S WHAT YOU DO

Spray-paint the typewriter red. The paint will overspray onto the keys. Let dry. With a small brush, paint the keys and other small areas gold. Let dry. Write a message on the paper with the marker and put in the typewriter.

Basket of Greetings

QUICK AS A WINK

Those wonderful Christmas card boxes of long ago may be empty, but they'll still bring a fulfilling smile displayed in a natural basket. We've stacked ours as full as can be, combining boxes from all generations and happy Christmases together for a wonderfully colorful holiday display.

Reindeer on Parade

Playtime Wreath

QUICK AS A WINK

Gather up all of those favorite toys of Christmases long ago and display them for all to see. Everyone will love to hear stories about your favorite holiday wishes that came true. We used fine wire to add this sweet collection to a fresh green wreath.

QUICK AS A WINK

Put a little light on your favorite collection. This collection of primitive tin items is given a little sparkle by using the pieces as candleholders. Be sure whatever you put the candles in will not burn.

Twinkling Tins

Time to Remember

QUICK AS A WINK

Choose your favorite collection to display on a large tray and embellish it all with old-fashioned icicles still available today. We chose this collection of clocks to display but other special stand-alone items such as Santas, angels, snowmen, or kittens, can be gathered together and adorned with the shiny icicles as well.

Memory Holder

Those treasured family pictures become pieces of artwork displayed on this unique photo holder. Choose a year that represents an important event in your family history to celebrate your special memories.

Here's What You Need
Tracing paper; pencil; scissors
12×4-inch piece of 1/2-inch pine; band saw
Sandpaper; black crafts paint; paintbrush
Drill; 1/8-inch drill bit; pliers; router
18 gauge black wire; thick wood glue
11 1/4 ×2 1/2-inch piece of 1/2-inch pine
(for base)

Here's What You Do
Enlarge and trace the desired number patterns, *right*, onto tracing paper. You may do this by using the grid or enlarging them 400% on a copy machine. Cut out the patterns and draw around them on the 12×4-inch piece of pine. Cut out the numbers using a band saw. Sand lightly; paint the numbers black. Allow to dry. Sand the edges for a worn look. Drill a 1/8-inch hole in the top of each of the numbers. Cut two 12-inch lengths of wire for each number. Twist wires together using pliers. On one end, make a double loop to hold the photo. For the number base, route three 1/2-inch channels 1/4-inch apart lengthwise. Paint the base black. Let dry; sand for a worn look. Decide where the numbers will be placed. Slide them into the routed channel and secure with wood glue. Put the wires in the hole in the top of the number with the double loop at the top.

0 1 2 3
4 5 6
7 8 9

1 SQUARE = 1 INCH

Lights on Display

QUICK AS A WINK

Those wonderful old Christmas lights and decorations of Grandma's can be your latest decorating accent when you add a few greens and display them prominently for all to see. We used old bubble lights from the 1950s and put them in a colorful antique Christmas lighting box.

Wreath of Ice Skates

Ice skating at Christmas time is a part of holiday memories for so many. Find those old worn out ice skates and turn them into a work of art by painting them with gold spray paint and acrylic paints. Display them in a fresh evergreen wreath adorned with tiny ornaments and curling ribbon for all to enjoy.

Here's What You Need

Small ice skates
Spray primer
Masking tape; gold spray paint
Acrylic paints in desired colors
Paintbrushes
Disposable foam plate
Spray varnish or sealer
Gold curling ribbon
Large fresh evergreen wreath
Small ornaments
Wide gold ribbon
Monofilament thread

Here's What You Do

Spray the skates with a spray primer. This will help paint stick better especially if skates are made from a slick vinyl.

When the primer is dry, mask off the edge of the lower portion of skates next to the blades using masking tape. Spray-paint the bottom of the skates including the blades with gold spray paint. Let the paint dry. Remove tape.

Begin painting the skates in any pattern and colors you wish. Follow the seams on the skates as a guide to break up colors. Paint background areas in solid pieces first, then add stars, dots, or circles. Paint the lace-ups a contrasting color. Allow the paint to dry. Spray with spray varnish. Allow to dry.

Lace up the skates with gold curling ribbon. Wrap the wreath with the same curling ribbon and add small ornaments and a bow if desired. Tie the painted ice skates into the wreath using the monofilament thread.

More Ways to Remember

There's no better time than Christmas to look back and recollect the best holidays of all. Here are some ideas for remembering days gone by and creating some new memories for your family.

🍂 Place photographs from past holidays under the glass in a serving tray. Display upright or use when guests come calling.

🍂 As you trim the tree, take turns telling favorite Christmas memories. Let the little ones tell about their favorite Christmas as Grandma tells of one long ago.

🍂 Keep a "favorite gift" book. Each year, describe the gift you enjoyed receiving the most and who gave it to you. Record what gift you liked giving the most and why.

🍂 When guests come to visit or when you have a party, place a guest book by the door. It's fun to look back and see who joined you to celebrate each year.

❧ Find favorite childhood treasures such as toys, books, and dolls, and place them under the Christmas tree to embellish those unopened packages.

❧ Purchase a set of sleigh bells at an antiques shop. Shake the bells outside the children's bedrooms on Christmas Eve to make unforgettable memories.

❧ Have older relatives write down or record remembrances they have about past holidays. Read or listen to them with your children.

❧ Treat yourself to a new Christmas crafts book. Spend an afternoon teaching a child or friend a new crafting technique.

❧ Keep a history of each Christmas tree ornament. List when it was received, where purchased, or from whom it was received.

❧ Find a favorite vintage holiday book and read it to your children or grandchildren and start a new tradition.

❧ Bring out antique quilts or quilt tops to use as tablecloths, tree skirts, or to hang behind the Christmas tree.

❧ Gather together three or four of Grandma's pressed-glass bowls in various sizes and heights. Arrange the bowls on the buffet filled with old-fashioned ribbon candies, peppermints, and large colorful gumdrops.

index

acknowledgements

Special thanks to B.J. Berti and Jim Blume who shared their creative ideas, opinions, and support in the making of this book.

GRAPHIC DESIGNER Angie Hoogensen specializes in book and magazine design. Her extraordinary sense of color and space are evident in all of her well-designed projects. She lives with her husband and three children and works from her craftsman-style art studio.

ARTIST Alice Wetzel is an accomplished book and magazine illustrator. Her versatile style ranges from whimsical to elegant as she combines various media to produce rich textures and colors.

PHOTOGRAPHER Pete Krumhardt is best known for his work photographing gardens around the world. His talents, however, extend to other subjects including home interiors, arts and crafts, and food photography. His creative use of lighting and his vast understanding of life and nature is apparent in all of his work. His work appears in a wide range of printed publications and on the internet.

PHOTOGRAPHER Andy Lyons is known for his creative work photographing children and adults as well as crafts, food, and decorating subjects. His unique and imaginative approach to every new project makes him a much-sought-after photographer across the United States. His work can be seen in a host of printed publications, including leading magazines and books as well as on the internet.

Models for this book were:

Ryan Banker, Jack Bender, Elizabeth Dahlstrom, Brennan DeJong, Krista DeJong, Laurel Hoogensen, Sarah Voy, and Alice Wetzel.

While all of the projects and recipes in this book have been checked and tested, human error can occur. Carol Field Dahlstrom, Inc. and Brave Ink Press cannot be held responsible for any loss or injury associated with the making of any item in this book.

THIS BOOK IS IN MEMORY OF MY FATHER WHO TAUGHT ME THAT EVERY DAY CAN BE LIKE CHRISTMAS.